IDIOT'S GUIDES

AS EASY AS IT GETS!

D0127482

Dog Tricks

by Deb M. Eldredge, DVM, and Kate Eldredge

Photography by Beth Adams

ALPHA

A member of Penguin Group (USA) Inc.

ALPHA BOOKS

Published by Penguin Group (USA) Inc.

Penguin Group (USA) Inc., 375 Hudson Street, New York, New York 10014, USA • Penguin Group (Canada), 90 Eglinton Avenue East, Suite 700, Toronto, Ontario M4P 2Y3, Canada (a division of Pearson Penguin Canada Inc.) • Penguin Books Ltd., 80 Strand, London WC2R 0RL, England • Penguin Ireland, 25 St. Stephen's Green, Dublin 2, Ireland (a division of Penguin Books Ltd.) • Penguin Group (Australia), 250 Camberwell Road, Camberwell, Victoria 3124, Australia (a division of Pearson Australia Group Pty. Ltd.) • Penguin Books India Pvt. Ltd., 11 Community Centre, Panchsheel Park, New Delhi—110 017, India • Penguin Group (NZ), 67 Apollo Drive, Rosedale, North Shore, Auckland 1311, New Zealand (a division of Pearson New Zealand Ltd.) • Penguin Books (South Africa) (Pty.) Ltd., 24 Sturdee Avenue, Rosebank, Johannesburg 2196, South Africa • Penguin Books Ltd., Registered Offices: 80 Strand, London WC2R 0RL, England

International Standard Book Number: 978-1-61564-767-5
Library of Congress Catalog Card Number: 2014957359

17   16   15   8   7   6   5   4   3   2   1

Interpretation of the printing code: The rightmost number of the first series of numbers is the year of the book's printing; the rightmost number of the second series of numbers is the number of the book's printing. For example, a printing code of 15-1 shows that the first printing occurred in 2015.

Printed in China

Note: This publication contains the opinions and ideas of its authors. It is intended to provide helpful and informative material on the subject matter covered. It is sold with the understanding that the authors and publisher are not engaged in rendering professional services in the book. If the reader requires personal assistance or advice, a competent professional should be consulted. The authors and publisher specifically disclaim any responsibility for any liability, loss, or risk, personal or otherwise, which is incurred as a consequence, directly or indirectly, of the use and application of any of the contents of this book.

Most Alpha books are available at special quantity discounts for bulk purchases for sales promotions, premiums, fund-raising, or educational use. Special books, or book excerpts, can also be created to fit specific needs. For details, write: Special Markets, Alpha Books, 375 Hudson Street, New York, NY 10014.

Trademarks: All terms mentioned in this book that are known to be or are suspected of being trademarks or service marks have been appropriately capitalized. Alpha Books and Penguin Group (USA) Inc. cannot attest to the accuracy of this information. Use of a term in this book should not be regarded as affecting the validity of any trademark or service mark.

PUBLISHER
Mike Sanders

EXECUTIVE MANAGING EDITOR
Billy Fields

EXECUTIVE ACQUISITIONS EDITOR:
Lori Hand

DEVELOPMENT EDITOR
Kayla Dugger

DESIGNER
Laura Merriman

PRODUCTION EDITOR
Jana M. Stefanciosa

INDEXER
Mary Harper

LAYOUT TECHNICIAN:
Brian Massey

PROOFREADER
Margaret Mincks

Contents

Part 2: Easy Tricks   50

Introduction

Looking for a fun way to bond and interact with your dog? Welcome to *Idiot's Guides: Dog Tricks!* Training tricks gives your dog special skills for play and everyday life, as well as strengthens your bond with your dog.

We start out in **Part 1, Training Basics,** by going through the basics of dog training and the foundation skills you and your dog will need to know as you go on to learn tricks. We use two positive training techniques throughout the book: shaping and luring. Both of these methods are described in detail here, and you and your dog can try each of them out. We generally explain how to teach each trick using one method or the other, but you can easily modify the training process to use the method that works best for you and your dog. As long as you are both having fun, there is no "wrong" way to train tricks.

We then get into the tricks themselves. The tricks are divided into three parts: **Part 2, Easy Tricks; Part 3, Intermediate Tricks;** and **Part 4, Advanced Tricks.** Easy tricks are simple to teach and can be done by just about any dog. Tricks categorized as intermediate level are either more intricate, somewhat physically challenging for either the dog or the handler, or require some extra effort to train. Advanced tricks are the most challenging and often include multiple parts and/or props. Depending on your dog's personal talents and preferences, these categorizations may not always hold true. Each dog is an individual, and some find learning tricks like Soccer to be much easier than learning Shake! Feel free to jump around the book and try the tricks that most appeal to you and your dog.

Within the parts, the tricks are mostly arranged to put similar tricks together. For example, paw tricks are grouped together, scenting tricks are together, and sports are together.

Each trick has step-by-step instructions along with photos to illustrate each step. We hope the photos help you to understand what we describe in the text and enable you and your dog to progress quickly and easily.

You also get various sidebars throughout the book. Dog Treat gives extra hints and tips for how to train a trick, while Pet Pause provides warnings for safety concerns or other things to think about before diving into a trick. There are even assorted sidebars that give info on alternative training methods, more advanced versions of the trick, and some ways to get creative and make a trick yours.

We hope you and your dog enjoy your trick-training journey!

But Wait! There's More!

Have you logged on to idiotsguides.com lately? If you haven't, go there now! As a bonus to the book, we've included additional information about dog tricks you'll want to check out, all online. Point your browser to idiotsguides.com/dogtricks, and enjoy!

Acknowledgments

We offer a huge thank you to all of the people and dogs that made this book unique: our intrepid and talented photographer, Beth Adams of Candid Canine Photography; Jamie Baker with Risa; Sue DeRienzo with Benny and Taxi; Meg Donley with Hobbes; Tom Eldredge with Baloo; Odette Fetzner with Cruise; Cindy Foley with Aries; Nancy Frakes with Josh and Merit; Ellen Griffin with Rosie and Saki; Robyn Haskin with Cooper; Christopher "Kip" Wilson with Zoey; Deb's dogs Babe and Doc (and Dani helping at home); and Kate's dogs Lynah and Queezle. Thanks also to Mike Basedow, the creator of the Nose trick.

And, of course, thank you to our production team: Kayla Dugger, Lori Hand, Laura Merriman, and everyone behind the scenes at Alpha Books.

We would like to dedicate this book to the great trick dogs of our past—Gus, Flash, Tia, and Hokey—who taught us so much.

Dog Profiles

We would like to introduce the 17 trick dogs who modeled tricks for this book. Any dog is capable of learning tricks, regardless of what breed or mix of breeds it is, so don't be discouraged if you don't see your dog's breed pictured. These are just a handful of the talented dogs in the world.

Merit

2-year-old Border Collie

Merit thinks the best thing to do is to cuddle on the couch with her human mother. Why work?

Hobbes

4-year-old Parson Jack Russell

Hobbes's favorite sports are running, agility, hiking, doing tricks, and swimming. He prefers to work for high-quality treats. Steak, anyone?

Baloo

12-year-old Australian Shepherd

Baloo likes to chase other dogs with the hose and play in the wading pool. He can even blow bubbles!

Queezle

9-year-old Belgian Tervuren

Queezle is a diva who loves to be groomed. She loves to compete in a wide variety of dog sports with owner Kate, and in her spare time steals food off the counter and barks out the window.

Cooper

6-year-old Nova Scotia Duck Tolling Retriever

Cooper is a multiple Best of Breed winner at the Westminster Dog Show and one of the top conformation Tollers for the past five years. He also has titles in obedience, rally, and hunting.

Babe

3-year-old Belgian Tervuren

Babe is as cute as a button and known as Deb's "personal pocket Terv." She loves herding both sheep and ducks and smacking her Easy button. Playing fetch and foot games are two of her favorite pastimes.

Benny

7-year-old Border Collie

Swimming is Benny's favorite activity—he loves his swimming pool. He also loves to compete in agility.

Aries

6-month-old Papillion

Aries loves food! He will work for food—any kind, anyplace, anytime. You bring the food, he will bring the trick.

Saki

1-year-old White Bull Terrier

Saki likes being busy—both good busy and "bad" busy! She thinks her tricks are the best, especially Get in a Box.

Risa

10-year-old mix

Adopted from a shelter when she was 2½ years old, Risa now competes in musical freestyle, rally, and obedience. Her mottos are "If it moves, chase it!" and "Never act your age. You can be a puppy forever."

Cruise

3-year-old German Shorthaired Pointer

Cruise competes in conformation, obedience, rally, agility, lure coursing, retriever hunt tests, and his personal favorite—pointer hunt tests. He's always been a happy guy who tries hard and is easy to train.

Lynah

2-year-old Belgian Tervuren

Lynah is a sweetie who loves to destroy toys and play with owner Kate. On the weekends she is a show dog, but during the week she sleeps on the bed and hides under Kate's desk with her toys.

Taxi

2-year-old Border Collie

Chasing—or rather, herding!—squirrels and bunnies is Taxi's passion. She loves learning clever tricks, too.

Rosie

2-year-old Colored Bull Terrier

Rosie loves to watch out the window for squirrels. She wonders why she didn't have a trailer and makeup artist for her photo shoot.

Josh

5-year-old Border Collie

Bringing toys to his human for play and trading is Josh's game. His person is well trained.

Zoey

11-year-old Boston Terrier

Zoey may be one of the oldest dogs in this book, but that doesn't slow her down. She loves to play soccer and will bark at her human teammates if they don't kick the ball high enough!

Doc

2-year-old Belgian Tervuren

Doc is named for the Bugs Bunny catchphrase "What's up, Doc?" That is his approach to life. He loves treats (except baked goods) and really enjoys tracking and herding sheep and ducks. Owner Deb is the love of his life.

PART 1:
Training Basics

Why Do Tricks?

Trick training is a great way to bond with your dog and make him a better companion. A trick can be as simple as shaking paws or as complex as bringing you a tissue when you sneeze. There is no pressure to be perfect or to learn every trick, so you can choose different tricks according to what you and your dog enjoy. Tricks also teach your dog important manners for everyday life in a no-pressure way.

There are many other reasons this kind of teamwork is good for both your dog and you—all of them positive!

For Your Dog

Dogs love tricks! Dogs, young and old, enjoy the mental stimulation of learning new things. Providing mental stimulation keeps an old dog sharp, disproving the idea that "you can't teach an old dog new tricks." When it comes to a puppy, the combination of having to think through tricks and doing them helps wear him out by giving him both mental and physical exercise.

Tricks also tend to be low-stress training. A session of trick training can be a relief to a dog who is going through a stressful transition (such as moving) or has anxiety issues. So unless you want to be on a reality TV show, there's no pressure doing tricks!

Plus, tricks often make your dog use unusual parts of his body or use his body in new ways, which can help him stay limber and fit. Stretching for a high five or bending around to do a spin makes your dog practice some new physical moves.

For You

It's not just your dog who benefits from dog tricks; teaching your dog new tricks and learning what works best for him is good for you, too.

Want a great stress reliever? Teach your dog to roll over! It is almost impossible to watch a dog roll over and not smile or laugh. Your dog's obvious enjoyment while performing his tricks will spread to you, even on a bad day.

You also get some mental stimulation of your own by coming up with fun variants on standard tricks. This kind of thinking and planning will make you a better trainer and improve your communication with your dog.

DOG TREAT

Most dogs have quite a sense of humor and will pick up on laughter and amusement when they do something cute. You may even find your dog adding his own flourishes to some tricks. For example, dogs are notorious for adding drama to a trick like Bang-Bang, You're Dead.

For Both of You

Working together to learn new tricks is a great way to build teamwork. Any type of training helps to strengthen the human-animal bond, and learning tricks together is an easy and enjoyable way to do so. You can follow your dog's natural inclinations and talents to learn standard tricks and then make up some of your own together! As long as you are having fun, both you and your dog will be engaged with the learning process.

Also, doing tricks with your dog can turn into a way for both of you to connect with others in your community. When practicing at a park or pet supply store, other people will admire your dog's cleverness and the way that you and your dog work together—after all, everyone loves to see happy people and happy dogs. You may even find that the work you do with your dog inspires other dog owners to do more things with their own dogs.

Setting Expectations

As you know, training your dog to do tricks is all about teamwork and the bond between you and your dog. These are some things to keep in mind when choosing what tricks to teach your dog and when training your dog.

Safety

Choose only tricks that your dog is physically capable of doing without hurting himself. Many tricks, like Shake or Touch, are easy for any dog to do. Others, like Sit Pretty or Catch a Disc, can be dangerous for dogs who are overweight or simply don't have the physique for that type of motion (think Mastiff or Bassett Hound). Slender dogs like Greyhounds will have trouble with tricks like Roll Over simply because they don't roll well!

Also keep in mind your dog's age. Young puppies shouldn't do anything that could put stress on their joints. Teach the basics and simple tricks while your puppy is young, but wait until he is at least a year old to work on anything that involves leaping. Older dogs may also have trouble with some motions or behaviors. Stick to things that he can do without being in pain. However, never listen to anyone who says that old dogs can't learn new tricks! Older dogs love learning new things and spending time with you as much as any puppy.

Your Dog's Background

Your dog's genetic background will affect his learning style and how he interacts with you. For example, Border Collies and other breeds developed for herding were selected to work closely with humans and follow instructions. This makes them very eager to please and quick to pick up on things. The same goes for sporting breeds, such as Labrador Retrievers or Irish Setters. These breeds will watch you and be very attentive to your body language.

If you have a Working or Hound breed, such as a Siberian Husky or Foxhound, you may find the training process takes a little longer. These breeds were designed to work independently and do their jobs without much human input. Don't worry—they are just as smart as other dogs and can still learn tricks! The challenge for you will be figuring out what motivates your dog and choosing rewards that will keep him engaged and interested. He may also be more easily distracted by his environment, so try to have your training sessions in a peaceful location.

Mixed-breed dogs are ruled by genetics just as much as purebred dogs. Figuring out what breeds or types of breeds your dog is can help you to learn more about his behavior.

The Process

The most important thing about training tricks is that they are supposed to be fun. However, learning something new can be hard and mentally tiring. Instead of working on a new trick for an hour, work on it a little bit at a time throughout the day, like 5 minutes in the morning, 10 minutes in the afternoon, and 5 minutes after dinner. Short training sessions prevent your dog from becoming totally exhausted, and can also cut down on frustration for both you and your dog if he is having trouble figuring something out.

When your dog does have trouble learning the next step to a trick, be patient. Sometimes we get so excited about the finished product that we don't spend enough time on the earlier steps. If you or your dog ever starts to get frustrated, it is probably time to take a break. Ask him to do something easy so you can end your training session on a positive note, and then go for a walk and try again later or the next day. If he is still having trouble, try going back to an earlier step to make sure he really does know it.

In the end, there are no hard-and-fast "rules" to training tricks—do what works for you and your dog, and have fun!

DOG TREAT

Adult dogs that have never really been taught anything before may take longer to learn things initially. This is especially true if you are using a clicker to shape tricks (more on this later!), because this training method requires the dog to be creative and an active part of the process. Don't worry, he will figure it out!

Equipment

A lead, a collar, and rewards such as toys to play with or treats to eat are the tools you need to start teaching tricks. As you get to the more advanced tricks, you can add to your collection. For now, though, let's take a look at the basics for dog tricks.

Collar

You should ideally use a buckle collar for training tricks. This can be an actual buckle or a quick release–type fastener. Avoid chains, slip collars, and prong collars; you don't want to give a correction by accident while your dog is learning. If your dog tends to slip out of collars, you may need a limited-slip martingale-type collar; these slip tighter when the dog pulls, but the straps can't tighten all the way.

Leash

When it comes to leashes, think of your comfort first! Avoid chain leads and stiff plastic leads. A nice leather or nylon lead will fit comfortably in your hand without any rubs or burns. Retractable leads are generally too complicated to handle while also trying to teach your dog tricks. If you'd like a leash for distance work, though, a long line can be used.

Clicker

A clicker is a little plastic box with a mechanism that makes a "click" sound when you press on it. Clickers can also come in other shapes, such as a rounded base with a button. This small noisemaker serves to "mark" a behavior so your dog knows that what he just did was something you liked. Many pet supply stores carry them, and they can easily be purchased online.

Treats

Don't forget treats! These can be standard kibble or something special, such as cooked chicken. Keep in mind that treats shouldn't be more than 10 percent of your dog's daily diet. You don't want a chubby dog!

Toys

Toys also make great rewards and can be useful for some tricks. Tug toys are always popular, and a canvas or plastic bumper is great for teaching some fetch behaviors.

Target

A target is used to designate a place or location to your dog. Any small, flat object will work as a target. One handy household item that can be used as a target is a plastic lid. Choose a bright color so it is easy for you to find in your training bag.

 DOG TREAT

When you start training behaviors like Hold and Carry, look around for household items that are portable. A cardboard toilet paper roll or a straw (for small dogs) makes for an inexpensive tool that is easy for your dog to hold.

PART 1: TRAINING BASICS

Positive Methods

We recommend using positive methods to train your dog. The main point of positive training is that the trainer rewards the dog for good behavior, or doing something right, instead of correcting the dog for bad behavior, or doing something wrong. Dogs don't like to be yelled at or hit any more than people do, and they love being praised and getting rewards!

The two methods we focus on in this book are *shaping* (also known as "clicker training") and *luring*. Both of these methods are designed to reward your dog for doing what you want. In the next few pages, you'll learn about each of these methods in depth so you can see which one works best for you and your dog. In our experience, trick training often requires a little of both, and the exact method you use will vary depending on the nature of the trick and your dog's preferences.

With the right training and attention, your dog will enjoy training sessions and even look forward to them.

Training Dos and Don'ts

DO	DON'T
Use rewards, such as treats or toys.	Strike your dog.
Use a neutral or upbeat voice.	Use an angry or mean voice.
Focus on successes.	Focus on failures.

Shaping

Shaping is a fun method that turns training into a game by encouraging your dog to figure out what you want on his own. It's just like the game "hot and cold"—you're leading your dog to do certain actions in order to perform a trick.

How it Works

All tricks and behaviors can be broken down into steps that gradually increase in difficulty and complexity. Shaping is about gradually molding your dog's actions into the final trick.

While the first step for shaping may not look like the final product, it'll have great significance in creating the sequence you want your dog to follow. For example, the first step of Shake is for your dog to lift or move his paw. As soon as that paw moves even a millimeter, it is your job to "mark" that behavior and let him know he is doing something good (more on markers in a moment). It will take some repetitions before he figures out exactly what he was doing that was right. But once he starts to move his paw on purpose and frequently, you can start asking for more effort, such as lifting his paw completely off the ground.

What makes shaping fun is that your dog has to guess what you want him to do. At first, he may be shy about offering behaviors. Feel free to break down steps even more so you can reward your dog for minimal effort. And if he ever gets confused or isn't making progress, you can easily go back to an earlier step as a refresher and work back up.

As he gains confidence and realizes there is never a wrong answer—just behaviors that earn a reward and ones that don't—he will get more creative and proactive about trying new things. You can then be pickier about what he has to do to get a reward.

DOG TREAT

The big idea behind all types of training is operant conditioning—the process of making an animal (or person!) behave in a certain way or do a certain thing. Operant conditioning has four forms: positive reinforcement, positive punishment, negative reinforcement, and negative punishment. For the purposes of this book, you only need to understand positive reinforcement. Positive reinforcement is when a reward is given for doing something right, such as giving your dog a biscuit when he sits on command.

Using Markers

An important component of the shaping method is using markers. A marker is anything that tells your dog he is on the right track and that a reward is coming soon. The marker figuratively marks the exact moment when your dog is doing something good. For example, people have long used their voices as markers by saying something like "Yes!" or "Good!"

More recently, dog trainers have started using clickers to mark behaviors in a process known as *clicker training* (which you'll see referred to interchangeably with shaping throughout this book). A clicker is not a magical training genie; rather, it is just a tool you can use for marking correct behavior.

The nice thing about using a clicker is that it provides context to your dog. Every time you take out the clicker, your dog knows that you are ready to train and will start offering behaviors and thinking about what you have worked on previously. Once your dog has mastered a trick, you can stop using the clicker and just reward him for a job well done.

PET PAUSE

If your dog is afraid of the loud click noise of a clicker, get a quieter clicker or use a short phrase, such as "yes," as your marker. You can also make a click sound with your tongue as a substitute for using a clicker.

Giving the Clicker (or Other Marker) Meaning

Before you can get started teaching tricks, your dog needs to understand that the clicker is a good thing. The following are some steps you should take to get your dog acclimated to the clicker.

Click the clicker and immediately give your dog a treat. Repeat this process several times until he anticipates the treat when he hears the click.

Ask your dog to do something he already knows, like Sit or Down. When he obeys you, click and treat. Repeat this a couple times to emphasize that "doing the right thing = click = treat."

You are now ready to start teaching your dog new tricks!

Getting into the Groove of Shaping

A large part of the process of shaping is a waiting game. You, the trainer, need to be patient and wait for your dog to offer a behavior that is on the path to the finished product.

It may take a few training sessions before your dog truly understands that he needs to try new things before you click, and which things to repeat, even if the action is as basic as looking toward an object. As you continue training, he will get better at guessing what you want quickly.

Keep training sessions short, and always end on something that your dog does well. This will keep him excited about training and wanting to do more.

Pluses and Shortcomings of Shaping

Shaping results in great retention of behaviors because the dog has to think a lot during the training process. All of that brain activity paints a vivid picture in your dog's mind of what he is supposed to do for each trick, making shaping a great method for training your dog.

However, some tricks and behaviors can take a long time to teach through shaping because they have to be broken down into so many steps. Also, depending on your dog, some behaviors may be so unnatural to him that he might never offer them on his own. Using luring (discussed shortly) instead of shaping can speed up the process a little and show your dog exactly what you want.

When it comes to clicker training in particular, dogs can also get really wound up. This is especially true of young or high-energy dogs. These dogs are already extremely excited when they see the clicker and just get higher and higher as they keep offering behaviors but aren't figuring out the right one. A dog this worked up isn't going to learn anything, so it's best in these instances to put the clicker away to create a calmer training environment. You can use your voice as a marker instead, or figure out a way to teach the trick with luring.

Luring

Luring is a method of training in which you lure or guide your dog through the motion or action you want to teach him. The lure will often be a treat held in your hand, but you can also use a toy or anything else that your dog is interested in.

How It Works

For luring, you hold a treat in front of your dog. Most likely, he will immediately start snuffling it and trying to take it from you. If you move your hand, his nose should follow. You can then use his attraction to the treat to lead him around or to manipulate him into a specific position, such as Sit.

Eventually, you want your dog to perform on command without a treat or toy in his face showing him what to do. This is known as *fading the lure*.

To fade the lure, repeat luring the behavior several times. After some repetitions, your dog will start to do the trick on his own without you needing to move the treat or toy quite as much. This is the beginning of fading the lure. As he gets more reliable, you can then give him less and less guidance. Eventually, he will perform the trick while you just hold the treat or toy, leading to a point where you can try asking him to do it without the object out at all.

However, just because you are fading the lure doesn't mean you aren't going to reward your dog for doing a trick. He still needs to be told how great he is when he does a trick correctly. Keep some treats in your pocket or on a nearby table so you can reward him after he does a trick without a lure.

Pluses and Shortcomings of Luring

Luring doesn't require any training beforehand. All you need is something that your dog likes and then a way to use that item to guide your dog into the position or motion you are looking for. This method allows your dog to develop muscle memory for each trick as you repeat with the lure.

However, luring doesn't require as much mental focus, meaning it may take your dog a while to perform a behavior without any assistance. Fading the lure can also be difficult if your dog is both highly food motivated and doesn't have a high desire to please.

It can also be challenging to teach some behaviors through luring. For example, to lure Salute, you would have to lift your dog's paw onto his head, something that most dogs would not like. For these kinds of tricks, it's best to use shaping instead so he can learn to do it himself at his own pace.

DOG TREAT

If your dog isn't interested in the treat you've chosen for luring, find something that does interest him. This might be a higher-value treat, such as lunchmeat or steak, or a favorite toy.

Rewards

Eventually, doing tricks can become a reward in itself for your dog. However, while he is learning, he needs to be rewarded for his efforts. Think of rewards as his paycheck—every time your dog puts in a good effort, he earns something special.

When teaching a new trick, you reward your dog every time. Once he masters the trick, you can randomize rewards to keep him guessing. Randomizing these rewards keeps your dog interested and motivated because he knows that he will get a reward sooner or later, but prevents him from becoming dependent on them to perform.

The reward can be anything that makes your dog happy and eager to work, such as treats, praise, toys, or play. Some dogs have a favorite reward that always works, while for others you may find that a different reward works better for different situations. The next few pages take you through each type so you can decide what works best for you and your dog.

DOG TREAT

When using a clicker, always remember to click before rewarding your dog, not after. The click is supposed to mark exactly what your dog is doing right, and then you can give him a reward. The reason why you don't use the reward itself as a marker is because sound travels much faster than your hand ever will—plus, when your dog sees a treat on the way, he is thinking about that instead of the action that earned him the treat!

Treats

Many dogs are food motivated, which means they love food. Some dogs will work for their regular kibble, while others will hold out for something better like steak or cooked chicken breast when learning a trick.

You may decide to use better treats while teaching a difficult trick and then revert back to lesser treats once the trick is mastered.

When your dog makes a breakthrough on a tough trick, you can even give a "jackpot," or many small pieces of a great treat.

Food can also be used as a lure. Whatever the case, these food rewards will eventually be phased out of your dog's tricks to become only random rewards.

Praise

Praise is a reward that doesn't require any special equipment—just your voice or your touch.

Don't hesitate to use your voice and praise your dog liberally. Some dogs like a squeaky, silly voice, while others prefer soft, calming praise. Try both versions and see what works best for your dog.

When it comes to the words you use, most dogs respond favorably to *good* or *yes*. The s sound in *yes* intrigues many dogs and makes them happy and excited. However, feel free to try different words to let your dog know how brilliant he is.

Petting is another easy form of praise your dog is sure to appreciate. If your dog loves physical contact, he may prefer being petted to any other reward.

Toys

Some dogs will turn their nose up at the best steak but flip for a ball or tug toy. When used as a reward, play with your dog instead of handing him the ball and walking away in order to foster teamwork.

Tugging using a toy is one fun way to play with your dog. It can get a dog very excited and enthused, so make sure that you call the shots. When you say "Drop it" or "Give," your dog must drop his end and stop.

Balls and flying discs are wonderful rewards, too. Many dogs are relentless retrievers and will bring the ball or disc back happily even if they have to work to earn another throw. If your dog doesn't bring the ball or disc back reliably, however, use a different reward so your training sessions can be productive.

Play

While play may involve a toy, you can also play with your dog by running with him, wrestling, or playing tag. Some dogs like foot games, where you try to touch his paw and he pulls it away before you can, or he tries to hit your hand with his paw. Other dogs enjoy hide and seek—you hide and they find you.

PET PAUSE

Keep play calm and controlled—no biting or grabbing allowed. A few excited barks may be fine, but your dog should not bark nonstop. If he gets overexcited, stop the play and refocus.

PART 1: TRAINING BASICS

Cues

A cue or signal is how people give dogs commands to tell them what to do. These can be as simple as one spoken word, or as elaborate as a long phrase or complicated hand motion.

The following pages discuss the role of body language and terminology in cueing your dog. For each of the tricks in this book, we will give you the hand signal and/or verbal cue that we use, but you can also make up your own commands and signals. Some people like to train their dogs in a foreign language, and others may need to adjust for physical limitations of the handler. As long as your dog knows what your cue means, you are good to go.

 DOG TREAT

When teaching your dog something new, be aware of words and motions that he already associates with other behaviors. For example, one of the most common causes of confusion for dogs is the phrase "Sit down." For a dog who knows both how to Sit and how to Down, this command makes no sense. Do you want him to Sit or to Down? To avoid this sort of confusion and frustration, keep your commands and signals clear and consistent for each trick so your dog can easily understand what you are asking of him.

Body Language

Body language includes any motion of your body—and we mean any. Dogs are very good at reading body language, and highly interactive dogs can respond to motions as subtle as a flick of your eyes or a change in your posture. Because of this sensitivity, it is your job to be aware of what signals you are sending and how they might impact your dog's behavior.

Posture

Posture is the most basic part of body language. One thing your posture does is tell your dog what kind of mood you are in and how you're feeling. Therefore, it is best to train when you are happy and relaxed, with loose shoulders and fluid movements. Your dog will read these signs and know that he can be happy and relaxed, too.

You can also use your posture and body movements to help your dog out when he is confused. Try leaning toward the place that you want him to go or the object that you want him to touch. Through this, your dog should figure out what you want very quickly.

Hand Signals

Hand signals are also key to training your dog using your body language. When using hand signals, make sure you are clear and consistent. For example, you want the hand motion you use to signal your dog to do Roll Over today to be the same one you use tomorrow.

It's also important to differentiate signals as much as possible. The signals for High Five and High Ten are very similar, so your dog will need to learn to pay attention to the voice command as well as your hand signals (we'll talk more about vocal cues shortly).

When performing hand signals, do them slowly enough that your dog has plenty of time to process what you want him to do. This is especially true when just starting on a new trick. As your dog gets better at the trick, he will recognize the signal faster, allowing you to give the signal more quickly.

Performing a trick in a new place or in front of people may also require you to slow down your signals some again. This helps both you and your dog overcome any nerves that could cause a communication breakdown.

Combating Mixed Signals

Bringing posture and hand signals together is crucial to conveying to your dog what you want him to do. Humans rely heavily on pointing, but dogs also read foot direction, where people's shoulders are facing, and eye motions. Leaning can also affect how your dog moves.

For example, if you are trying to get your dog to move in one direction but he keeps doing something else, check to make sure your whole body is sending the same message. You may be pointing at a toy to your left for your dog to pick up, but if your body is leaning to the right, he may go right. One easy way to combat this is to make eye contact and then move your eyes to look at the object that you want him to touch, repeating a couple times as necessary.

In the end, always consider what your body is telling your dog, especially when working on something that includes directional movements.

DOG TREAT

If you are ever around a group of dogs, watch how they interact with each other. Even though they don't talk like we do, a lot of silent communication goes on. Watching how dogs communicate can help you to understand your dog and how he sees the world.

Verbal Cues

Humans talk a lot. We gossip with our friends, we argue on the phone, and we chatter at our dogs. Our dogs have to sift through all of this noise and pick out the words that actually apply to them. So what's important when cueing your dog verbally?

Tone

If you pay attention to other dog owners, you will notice that they all have a special tone of voice they use when giving their dogs commands. It is usually authoritative without being angry.

This firm voice is perfect for telling your dog what to do next, because it differs from your playtime voice and scolding voice. These differences in tone are why your dog will sit when you tell him to, but not when you ask your friend if she would like to sit.

Clarity

Clarity is another thing to consider for verbal cues. When selecting words for your commands, choose ones that sound unique. For example, the similarity of the sounds in "Down" and "Bow" can cause confusion for your dog. To make the different cues clearer, either use a different word for one of the tricks (some people use "Ta-da!" for the Bow trick) or pronounce the two words clearly with emphasis on the sounds that are different (in other words, emphasize the *D* and *B* rather than the *ow*).

Also, try to curb any babbling while training and performing. This is especially true if your dog is having trouble figuring something out. Keep commands simple, and don't surround them with other words that mean nothing to your dog.

Using Verbal Cues at the Right Time

A voice command should indicate a complete behavior. Therefore, you shouldn't use verbal cues until a trick has been at least partially mastered. For example, when you say "Spin," you want your dog to make a complete circle, not just turn his head.

Once you have added in the command for a trick, reward your dog for doing the trick only when you specifically asked for it by giving the command. This will increase the value of the command, because it becomes the necessary pass code for your dog to do the trick and get his reward. If he offers something without being asked, just ignore him and continue with your training.

DOG TREAT

For each of the tricks in this book, we will tell you the command that we use or the most common command for that trick. Feel free to get creative and use different words or languages—as long as you and your dog both understand what each word or phrase means, it doesn't matter if it doesn't make sense to anyone else!

Don't Overdo It

A good rule to follow with anything you teach your dog is to give a command only once. If he doesn't do Down on the first command, he probably won't on the fourth; that means either that he doesn't truly understand the command and behavior or that you have some teamwork issues to work through. Repeating your command endlessly only serves to lessen its value.

To deal with this issue, review the trick and make sure your dog understands it. If he has mastered a trick, reward him only if he does it the first time you ask. If he does not, say something like "Nope, no cookie for you," and break off the session.

A useful way to create a lot of interest and motivation in understanding your verbal cues is to either give the treat or other reward to another dog (if you have one) or to pretend to eat the treat yourself when your dog doesn't follow your command. This shows your dog that if he doesn't play by the rules, he can't have the prize, and even worse, someone else is getting the prize. You can then work on something else before coming back to the trick he resisted and see whether he's now paying attention.

PART 1: TRAINING BASICS

Basic Skills

The behaviors we teach you how to train in this section are all used as part of the foundation for other tricks. They are also good skills to have for life with your dog in general!

We start off with the true basic commands that every dog should learn: Sit and Down. These positions are both great starting points for other tricks and are also useful anytime you need your dog to be under control, such as waiting at the veterinarian's office or greeting new people.

We then go on to actions involving objects like toys or other props—Fetch, Drop It, Give, Hold, and Carry. You can use these commands both when playing with your dog and for training tricks that involve an object your dog will need to pick up and do something with.

You then learn how to teach Leave It and Wait, which are both extremely useful life skills that give your dog better self-control. They are especially good for when your dog is around food, open doors, or other exciting things.

Finally, we cover Targeting, which is used in teaching several tricks. The target indicates to your dog where he needs to focus his attention.

Sit

A solid Sit can be used as the basis for many tricks and to simply make sure your dog is focused on you. It is also an excellent life skill, allowing him to sit to greet people politely, sit patiently at doors, and so on.

Sit may seem like a very basic behavior, but that is what makes it the perfect start for training. All dogs sit. Your goal is to get your dog to sit on cue. Because this is a common dog behavior, you may choose to shape this trick—simply wait until you see your dog start to sit, and then click and treat. Alternatively, this is an easy trick to start with luring. The following are the steps for luring Sit.

Hold a treat (or a toy, if your dog prefers that) slightly above your dog's head so he reaches for it with his nose. Make sure your hand is closed so he won't get the treat.

Move your hand back and over his head, toward his tail. As he lifts his head to follow the treat, he should start to lower his hindquarters.

DOG TREAT

Use treats until you feel your dog knows both the hand cue and the word of the trick. Once your dog has shown he understands the behavior, you can then start to randomize your rewards. Sometimes, give him a treat the first time he sits on command; other times, ask him to do a couple repetitions before giving him a treat. This will prevent him from being dependent on food to perform. Always praise and/or pet every time your dog does a correct behavior; after all, those are rewards you will always have with you!

Maneuver the treat so he drops into a sitting position. Praise and reward. At first, you may need to gently guide his rear down with your other hand; however, never force him to sit. Repeat several times so your dog starts to associate the treat and hand motion with the action of sitting.

As he becomes proficient, add in the word "Sit" before you give the signal. You can choose to fade out the hand cue and just use the word or keep your dog on his toes by alternating which cue you use.

Down

The Down position is a handy skill for every dog to know. It is the basis for some tricks like Roll Over and Bang-Bang, You're Dead. Down also means your dog is under control and in a safe location, which can save the day when you stop for ice cream at an outdoor café after a training session—you get ice cream, while your dog enjoys a bowl of fresh water lying at your feet!

You can shape this behavior by watching when your dog is tired and clicking as he goes to lie down, but luring is a quicker method for most dogs, as shown in the following steps. A larger dog can easily learn this while on the ground. However, if you have a small dog or young puppy, you can use a grooming table or other safe surface to train him to put less strain on your back.

Start with your dog in a standing position. Bring a treat up to his nose so he reaches for it.

Bring the food down directly in front of your dog. This leads his nose to follow the food, causing his neck to bend. Plus, by holding the food with your palm down, you are also incorporating a hand signal for this behavior.

PET PAUSE

Some dogs may need gentle pressure on their rear end if they try to stop with their rear up and only their front down. However, do not get into a pushing match! If your dog resists, start over on a slippery surface so your dog will slide into the Down position.

Continue to bring the food down, moving it back between your dog's front legs. As his nose follows the food down and back, his front legs will extend and his body will start to drop, until he lets himself go totally down.

Praise and reward! Repeat several times until he starts to anticipate and go down with less maneuvering from you. You can then add in the word "Down" before giving him the signal to drop. As with Sit, you can gradually fade the hand signal and just use the word or alternate between the two cues.

Fetch

Fetch can be used both for formal tricks and for just having fun with a toy in your yard. Practice shaping this with several different objects or toys—such as a dumbbell used in obedience training, a rolled-up newspaper, or a ball—to diversify your dog's talents and to make sure he truly understands the behavior.

Get an object that your dog can safely and easily pick up and place it on the ground. Click and treat if your dog looks at or moves toward it. Repeat several times.

Click and treat if he actually touches the object. At first, you can reward if he touches it with either a paw or his nose, but after a few reps, reward only for touching it with his nose. Repeat until he is doing this frequently.

DOG TREAT

If you are having trouble shaping your dog to Fetch on command, you can try teaching this behavior by tuning in to your dog's natural prey drive and chase instinct. Get your dog excited about the toy by waving it around and teasing him with it, and then toss it a short distance. He should run and grab it automatically. You can then encourage him to bring the toy back to you, either by patting your leg or running in the opposite direction to get him to chase you. Once your dog brings the toy back to you, toss it again, giving your Fetch command as your dog runs after it. After several repetitions, your dog will connect your Fetch command with playing and bringing the toy back to you. Now that your dog is excited about fetching and understands the verbal cue, you can try the more formal retrieve.

Wait for your dog to grab the object. He doesn't have to totally pick it up yet—just start to. With a hard object, you may hear his teeth click on it. Repeat until he is touching the object just about every time.

Click and treat if your dog actually lifts the object, even just a little. This is one of the harder steps to get, so be patient. Repeat until he is consistently picking it up.

Move the object so it isn't right next to you and review the earlier steps with him. Click and treat for even one step toward you while he has the object in his mouth. Gradually add distance until he is bringing it all the way to you. You can now add in your command by saying "Fetch" or "Take it" before releasing him to go get the object.

Drop It and Give

These commands are used to tell your dog to release whatever he is holding in his mouth and let you take it. You will need them for tricks that involve retrieving or carrying objects, plus they are useful for playing with toys and those rare occasions when your dog picks up something that you don't want him to have!

We like to differentiate between Drop It and Give, so "Drop it" means the dog needs to just drop whatever he is holding and "Give" means he should literally give the object to you and release it into your hands. Feel free to only teach one or both, depending on what you would like your dog to do.

Drop It

This version is ideal for when you either do not want to touch whatever your dog is carrying (like a dead squirrel or slimy soccer ball) or it doesn't matter whether he delivers it to your hands.

Throw a toy for your dog or tug with him a little to get him interested in it. Try to take the toy from your dog. Praise and reward when he lets go.

Start telling him to "Drop it" before reaching for the toy. As you practice, he will start to anticipate and let go of the toy without the reminder from you. Reward him by throwing the toy again and playing some more.

Give

This version is ideal for when you want your dog to deliver something directly to your hands, such as when sitting in a chair while playing Fetch or when asking your dog to bring you something.

Get your dog interested in a toy. Try to take the toy from your dog. If he doesn't automatically release it, gently insert your finger into his mouth to encourage him to drop the toy. Praise and reward.

As you reach for the toy, say "Give." Reach your hands toward your dog's head to tell him you want to take the toy directly from him. Reward only if he releases the toy into your hands—not if he drops it on the ground.

DOG TREAT

If your dog doesn't automatically release the toy when you try to take it, gently insert your finger into his mouth. Most dogs will let go immediately for that. You can also put gentle pressure on the roof of his mouth to encourage him to drop the toy.

Hold

Hold is a necessary behavior for tricks that require your dog to hold onto an object. It can also come in handy for staging cute photos! You may find that your dog gets too excited about the clicker to focus on this behavior. If you get to a point where he isn't making progress, put the clicker away and just reward with praise and treats as you shape the behavior you want.

Hold an object in your hand, and click and treat when your dog moves his nose toward the object. Repeat several times until he is reaching for the object intentionally.

Click and treat if he actually touches the object with his nose. As he gets more confident, move the object around a little so he has to move different directions to reach it.

DOG TREAT

You can work on extending his hold time by reviewing Give and rewarding for Hold only if your dog continues to hold the object until you tell him to give it to you.

Click and treat when he grabs the object. You may be able to hear his teeth click on a hard object. Repeat until he is taking the object completely in his mouth.

Start enforcing an actual hold by waiting a second or two before rewarding, making sure not to reward if he grabs and immediately releases. You can help him figure this out by gently holding his mouth closed around the object. (Don't squeeze!)

Extend hold time. If you are using your hand as a reminder, try releasing pressure and moving your hand away a little bit at a time. When your dog can hold the object on his own for a few seconds, add in the command "Hold."

Carry

Carrying objects is a skill that can be difficult to teach because it is about maintaining rather than performing a specific action, such as picking up or putting down an object. You can approach it in two ways: as an extension of Hold or as a separate behavior.

As your dog learns this, note that just because he can carry his favorite tennis ball for hours doesn't mean that he will be able to do the same with something larger, such as a basket. Therefore, each time you ask him to carry a new object, you may need to start over at the beginning. He will improve more quickly as he figures out that Carry can apply to anything, not just one object or toy.

As an Extension of Hold

The plus to teaching Carry as an extension of Hold is that your dog already knows Hold and has that foundation. Adding motion will be challenging at first, especially as you start practicing outside with more distractions, but it will ultimately strengthen your dog's Hold.

To do this, review Hold with your dog. Next, clip the leash on your dog and try walking a few steps while reminding your dog to Hold. After those first few steps, praise and reward. Don't forget to tell him to "Drop it" or "Give" to release him from the hold.

You can then work up to walking around your house and yard without your dog dropping the object.

As a Separate Behavior

The plus to using this method for Carry is that the command has a specific context: a Hold in motion. This can be comforting to dogs (and people) who have trouble generalizing.

To start, tell your dog to Fetch an object, and then start walking as he tries to bring it to you. Praise and reward when he catches you. Repeat this process a couple times so he can get used to the game.

Now, after telling him to Fetch, give your Carry command; we recommend saying "Carry" or "Bring it." Praise and reward when he catches you. Don't forget to tell him "Drop it" or "Give" when he is allowed to release the object.

Once he has the hang of it, start extending the distance that he has to carry the object. Clip on your leash, tell him to pick up the object and to carry it, and walk a few steps before rewarding. Work up to walking around your house and yard without your dog dropping the object.

DOG TREAT

Holding on to something takes concentration enough; holding it while walking is even harder. Be patient as you work on this skill with your dog, and be sure to practice in different environments. Start easy in locations that are quiet and familiar, and then gradually take him to more interesting and exciting places.

Leave It

Leave It is another command that is useful both when training tricks and when simply out and about in the real world. In training, you can use it if you don't want your dog to go to a treat or toy right away; the rest of the time, it can be used to prevent your dog from stealing food or eating something bad for him. The ideal end result is that if your dog hears you say "Leave it," he will immediately avoid whatever he was looking at or trying to get.

Hold a treat in the palm of your hand. If your dog tries to steal the treat, close your hand around it so he can't grab it. If he licks your hand, keep it closed.

When your dog pulls away from your hand, try opening it again. It may take several tries before your dog stops trying to steal the treat. When he backs off, praise him and give him a different treat with your other hand. Once your dog understands that he can't take the treat in your hand, add in your Leave It command. Say "Leave it," and then present the treat on your open palm.

DOG TREAT

Why give your dog a different treat and not the one in your hand? This reinforces that the treat in your hand is off-limits, and that whenever your dog hears you say "Leave it," he absolutely can't steal that item. The other treat is a reward for making the right choice.

Try placing the treat on the floor and telling your dog to leave it. (If you're working outside, put the treat on a piece of paper so you can see it.) Be ready to cover the treat if he goes for it! Practice until he can be trusted to leave the treat alone.

Try walking past the treat on the ground with your dog while telling him to leave it, and set up other tests around the yard or room. This gives your dog practice with leaving treats alone in different areas.

Wait

Like Leave It, Wait involves your dog having self-control around exciting things, such as toys, people, or open doors. When used in trick training or on its own, a solid Wait can impress an audience. Outside of tricks, this skill teaches your dog good manners and even protects him from harmful objects or situations.

Initial Training Process

Although we teach Wait with shaping, we recommend not using a clicker, because it can be too exciting for many dogs and thus counterproductive. As far as formal steps go, there are only a couple.

First, praise for stillness. Your dog can be in any position, but we find Sit and Down to be easier to start out with. You can work on a stand later.

Next, gradually increase the length of time your dog has to hold his position before being praised and released. Work up to several minutes, and always use a release word to tell your dog when he is allowed to move again. Many trainers use "Okay!" or "Free!"

It is important not to reward your dog if he breaks his Wait before being released. If he does, just quietly put him back where he was supposed to be and try again.

DOG TREAT

Wait can be difficult for many dogs to learn because they are being rewarded for inaction rather than for doing something—this is confusing! Therefore, be patient with your dog and reward for even just a few seconds of staying still until he starts to get the idea.

Taking It Further

Once your dog has a reliable Wait at home, try it in other places. It probably won't be as good, but just go back and review the baby steps. He will get better at generalizing the more places you take him to practice. As with every other trick and behavior, start with calm, quiet places and gradually work up to exciting ones.

You can also practice having your dog do Wait at certain times or in certain situations, such as mealtimes, when you open a door to take him outside, and when you throw a toy for him. These are all very challenging and can take a while to perfect, but in the end you will have a well-mannered dog.

Targeting

Targeting is an easy way to focus your dog's attention on a specific place or location, whether it is close up or away from you.

Targets are used for two main things: adding distance and designating location. If you want your dog to do something away from you, you can send him to the target and then give him a command. If you want your dog to put his nose or paw in a certain spot, you can use the target as a point for him to hone in on.

As you learned earlier, a target should be a small, flat object. Many trainers use the lids from tubs of butter or other jars. You can also use a mouse pad or piece of cardboard (paper can be a temporary option, but we find that it doesn't hold up well to repeated use).

The following walks you through how to give a target meaning for your dog. We recommend teaching your dog to use both his nose and foot to touch the target; each of these will be useful later.

Place your target on the ground. Click and treat when your dog looks at or moves toward it.

Click and treat when your dog actually touches the target with his nose or paw. You can now add in your command—say "Target" and then reward your dog for touching the target. From here you can work on sending your dog to the target from a distance.

Go back and work on the opposite of what your dog has already learned. For example, if he originally chose to use his nose, teach him to use his paw.

DOG TREAT

No matter what you use your target for, you will eventually need to fade it out when your dog has mastered the behavior. An easy way to do this is to literally shrink the target over time. For example, if you're using a piece of paper or cardboard as a target, cut some of it away every day or so until nothing is left.

Taking Your Tricks on the Road

Other people enjoy seeing your dog's tricks as much as you do! Whether you are just showing off to your friends or doing a more formal performance at a park or nursing home, here are some tips for making the most of your performance.

Considering Your Dog

A social dog would love to perform his tricks at a nursing home or during a community function. If your dog loves kids, showing off at a school or summer camp event could be a blast. However, dogs that are reactive or shy may find the idea of a public performance to be torture. Some of these dogs might enjoy doing a demo but prefer to skip the "meet, greet, and pet" that tends to follow.

Always be your dog's advocate, and make sure he is happy and comfortable.

Preparing Your Dog for Outings

If you feel your dog will have fun doing tricks in public, you still need to get him out and about to train in different places. Dogs do not generalize well, so you may find he completely forgets a trick that he does perfectly at home when you ask him to do it somewhere else.

Start by taking your dog to places that allow dogs but are fairly quiet. Many pet supply, home supply, and camping/outdoor gear stores will allow dogs in. Keep your dog calm around customers, store staff, and any other dogs, and always obey leash laws.

You can begin your work in the new environment by practicing basic tricks that your dog is confident about. You may have to help him with extra cues or a lure at first. Have some of your dog's favorite treats or his best toy with you as rewards. Plan on working for just five minutes at first, and then head out and give your dog a fun break.

As your dog gets more comfortable in these environments, try practicing in places that are busier and more exciting, like parks or near an outdoor café.

Never hesitate to give your dog extra help. It can be hard to concentrate with new distractions. Even if he acts like he has never done a trick before in his life, remain positive. He will settle and work once he has a chance to check everything out. If he does not settle down to work after a couple of outings, go back to practicing at home and possibly reassess if public performances are something your dog will enjoy.

Where to Go

If you're looking for places your dog can show off his tricks, many communities have dog education days either in conjunction with the AKC Responsible Dog Owners program or through local shelters and rescues. A trick class competition may even be offered. These events often have associated fundraisers to benefit homeless pets or raise money for canine health research, allowing you and your dog to have fun and do some good for the dogs of the world at the same time.

Certification through an established therapy dog group can open up opportunities for you and your dog to visit nursing homes, senior activity centers, and schools.

Keeping Your Sense of Humor

One of the most important things about doing trick performances with your dog in public is to keep your sense of humor. The people watching already think your dog is incredible because he is out in public and behaving, so they may not realize a trick is falling apart even though you are quickly becoming embarrassed. Just think quickly on your feet and cover for your dog. For example, what do you do if you try Bang-Bang, You're Dead and your dog remains standing, looking at you? A couple of answers could be, "Oh no, I must be out of ammunition!" or "Oh no, it is Super Dog, and the bullets are just bouncing off of him!" You can then laugh and get your dog to play or do a very simple trick. People will enjoy your dog's bloopers as much as, or more than, his perfect performances.

PART 2:
Easy Tricks

Touch

Verbal Cue	Prerequisites
"Touch"	None
Hand Signal	Tools
	None

Touch is a very simple trick, making it the perfect one to start out with when training your dog. Once your dog has learned Touch, you can use it to get her focused on you in a busy area or as a warm-up before working on other tricks.

DOG TREAT

As well as using your hand, you can also teach your dog to touch your foot or the end of a stick.

Hold your hand out flat with your palm facing your dog, and click and reward when she looks at it. Repeat a few times to help her figure out what she's doing right.

Click and reward when your dog reaches for your hand with her nose.

3 Wait until her nose makes contact with your hand to click and reward. You can now add in the verbal cue "Touch," and then offer your hand. Click and reward when she touches it.

4 When your dog has mastered touching your hand at the verbal cue, try moving your hand around or asking her to touch your other hand.

TAKING IT FURTHER

Depending on your dog's age and physical ability, you can even ask her to jump to touch your hand. Start out with your hand low, and then gradually raise your hand. Don't forget to reward her for a job well done!

Nose

Verbal Cue	Prerequisites
"Nose"	None
Hand Signal	Tools
	None

Nose is a slightly more involved version of Touch. This trick is simple and silly, and perfect for dogs with long noses! Because you will need both hands for the signal, this trick can't be taught with a clicker. Instead, use your voice as a marker.

! PET PAUSE

This trick may be difficult to do with a dog that has a very large or smushed muzzle, especially if you have small hands. Feel free to modify the hand signal to adjust to your dog's needs, such as holding your hands apart rather than having your fingertips touching.

1

Place your hands together in the shape of a triangle, as shown in the hand signal. Your hands should be held low enough that your dog can easily reach them. Praise and reward when your dog looks at your hands or moves toward them.

2

Praise and reward when your dog touches your hands with her nose.

3

Wait until your dog sticks her nose, even a little bit, in the space between your hands to praise and reward. Repeat a couple times until she is doing this consistently and not missing and hitting your hands with her nose.

4

Require her to put her nose all the way through your hands to get a reward. Add in your verbal cue by saying "Nose" before offering her your hands.

DOG TREAT

Hold your hands low enough that your dog can easily reach her nose between them. If you are holding them too high, she might not be able to reach! For smaller dogs, you may need to kneel or put your dog on a raised surface.

Once your dog has mastered the trick, you can try having her jump to reach your hands. As always with jumping, consider your dog's physical abilities and don't ask her to do something that might cause her to hurt herself.

Shake

Verbal Cue	Prerequisites
"Shake"	Sit
Hand Signal	Tools
	None

Shake is one of the most well-known and popular tricks. Everyone expects dogs to do this one! It is simple to train, especially with a dog who likes to use her paws.

TARGET METHOD

You can also teach this trick by using a target and holding it in your hand. Start low so your dog can easily reach the target, and then gradually work up until you are holding the target at a normal height for Shake. Once your dog is consistently hitting the target with her paw, fade the target until she's just putting her paw into your bare hand.

Put your dog in a Sit and watch for any movement of her paw. When you see any motion, click and reward. Repeat several times until she starts to move her foot on purpose, and gradually require her to lift her paw higher to make you click.

Hold your hand so your dog's paw will hit it accidentally. Click and reward when this happens. Reward only if her paw makes contact with your hand.

At this point, reward only when your dog's paw lands in your palm and stays there for a few seconds. Once the paw is reliably landing on your palm, you can add in your verbal cue by saying "Shake" before offering your hand.

DOG TREAT

Your dog may not be comfortable with having her paw caught and held at first. Therefore, be sure to give her lots of treats, and always hold her paw gently (don't squeeze!).

You can also just teach her to leave her paw in your hand for a few seconds instead of holding it. To do this, gradually extend the amount of time her paw has to remain in your hand before you click and reward. If your dog has a solid Wait, you can tell her to do that when her paw hits your palm as a hint. Once she figures out that you want her paw to stay in your hand, you will be able to stop using the Wait command, and the pause will be assimilated into Shake.

Wave

Verbal Cue	Prerequisites
"Wave"	Shake
Hand Signal	**Tools**
	None

Wave is a cute and simple trick that's perfect for when you want your dog to greet someone or say good-bye. Teaching Shake first can make the process go a little faster, but your dog does not have to know Shake to learn Wave.

DOG TREAT

Reward your dog only when she raises a single paw. If she hits you with her paw or jumps at you, just ignore her, and these behaviors will go away.

Click and reward if your dog moves or lifts her paw even a tiny bit. If you have already taught her Shake, you can hold your hand out (as if signaling Shake) to encourage her to raise her paw.

Gradually require her to raise her paw higher before you click. If you used your outstretched palm, move your hand higher and higher until it is at least at hip level. Repeat until she is consistently lifting her paw to the height you desire.

Add in your hand signal and verbal cue by waving at your dog and saying "Wave." Click and reward for the behavior.

CHANGING PAWS

To make your dog's Wave more impressive, you can teach her to use each of her paws based on which hand you wave at her with, using a different command for each paw. To do this, decide which paw and hand should go together, such as your left hand and your dog's left paw. When you wave at her with your left hand, reward only if she uses her left paw. You can then go back and teach her to use her right paw when you wave with your right hand.

One option for multiple commands is "Hello" for your dog's left paw and "Good-bye" for her right. You can also use "Wave" for the left paw and carry over "Shake" for the right because your dog will be using the same motion she does for Shake.

High Five

Verbal Cue	Prerequisites
"High five"	Sit, Target

Hand Signal	Tools
	Target (optional)

High Five is a variation of Shake. For this trick, you want your dog to raise her front leg high and slap your hand. This can be done with a target or by using your hand as a target.

PET PAUSE

Some dogs become overenthusiastic about this trick and may whack the hand presented to them. If your dog is like this, you can discourage excessive force by practicing when she is calm and only doing one or two repetitions. Reward only if she gives you a calm High Five. In the meantime, do not encourage small children or senior citizens to try out this trick with your dog. They could get injured.

Hold the target in your hand close to the ground and ask your dog to hit it with her paw. Click and reward. If she uses her nose instead, just ignore her.

Gradually raise your hand so your High Five gets higher. Go only as high as your dog can comfortably reach.

Flip your hand so your palm is facing toward your dog instead of under her paw; this will be her cue for High Five. Once the paw is reliably touching your raised palm, add in your verbal cue by saying "High five" before you give the hand signal.

DOG TREAT

Your dog can use either paw for High Five. Some dogs automatically prefer their right paw after learning Shake, but some trainers choose to differentiate between Shake and High Five by requiring High Five to be done with the left paw. Once your dog has learned the trick, you can use the verbal cue "High five" or use the palm facing your dog as the hand signal cue. Or do both!

Fade out the target by gradually making it smaller or by taking it away and only using it periodically if your dog seems confused. Some dogs will make the adjustment easily, while others will need some reminders.

High Ten

Verbal Cue	Prerequisites
"Gimme ten"	High Five
Hand Signal	Tools
	None

High Ten is perfect for when a High Five just isn't quite awesome enough. Because both of your hands are necessary for the hand signal for this trick, you will not be able to use a clicker. Instead, use your voice as a marker.

! PET PAUSE

Once you have added in your verbal cue, make sure you reward your dog for High Ten only when she is asked to do so. A surprise jump with both paws out could cause someone to get hurt, especially if you have a larger dog.

Hold both of your hands low to the ground, palms facing up. Praise and reward when your dog puts one of her paws on a hand. This gets her thinking about using her paws, so you need to do it only once or twice.

Wait until your dog puts both of her paws on your hands to praise and reward. You may need to give her some verbal encouragement to get her excited enough to jump up with both paws. Repeat until she is doing this consistently.

3

Flip your hands so your palms are facing your dog. Praise and reward when she hits your hands with both paws. Add in your verbal cue by saying "Gimme ten" before offering your hands.

ADDING A JUMP

Depending on your dog's size and athleticism, you can work up to asking your dog to jump to hit your hands!

Salute

Verbal Cue	Prerequisites
None	Sit
Hand Signal	Tools
	Scotch or masking tape

Salute is the perfect trick for national holidays or just showing some extra respect for your dog's elders. As you teach this, hold the clicker in your right hand (the one that you salute with) so you can still give your dog a treat with your left hand.

! PET PAUSE

This trick could be difficult for senior dogs who have some arthritis or for dogs with very short front legs.

Take a small piece of tape and place it on your dog's muzzle or head. Click and reward when your dog lifts her paw to rub off the tape. You can click for any raise of her paw, even if she doesn't touch her head.

Click and reward only if your dog touches her head or nose with her paw and is in a Sit or standing position. If she knocks the tape off, just replace it or get a new piece. Repeat until she is doing this consistently.

3

Add in your hand signal. Salute your dog, and then click and reward when she swipes the top of her head with her paw. At this point, you should reward only when your dog salutes on cue.

4

Fade the use of the tape. You may be able to stop using it all at once, but if not, use smaller and smaller pieces until you aren't using any at all.

TROUBLESHOOTING

Some dogs (such as our model) don't automatically try to knock the tape off their noses. If this is the case with your dog, make sure the tape is in a spot she can see and then gently touch it with your finger. The pressure makes it tickle, encouraging your dog to rub the tape with her paw.

Pray

Verbal Cue	Prerequisites
"Say your prayers"	None
Hand Signal	**Tools**
None	Chair

This trick is normally done using a human bed as the prop, but if you're training away from home (or if your dog isn't allowed on the bed), you can use a chair or box instead. For a small dog, choose a box appropriate for her size. Whichever object you use, the end goal is for your dog to place her front paws on top of it and then rest her head between her paws as if she is saying her prayers.

DOG TREAT

You can also use a lure or place a target between your dog's paws to encourage her to lower her head.

Click and reward when your dog touches the chair with either her nose or paw (if using a bed or box, she can touch the side of it at this step). Work up to only rewarding when she uses her paw.

Wait for your dog to put her paw on top of the chair to click and reward. Repeat until she is placing her paw on top of the chair every time.

Require your dog to put both front paws on the top of the chair. Click and reward, and repeat until she is doing this consistently.

When both of your dog's paws are in position, click and reward if she dips her head toward her paws. Reward for any dip at this step.

Work up to your dog lowering her head to rest on or between her paws. You can now add your verbal cue by saying "Say your prayers" before she puts her paws up and head down.

Watch

Verbal Cue	Prerequisites
"Watch me"	None
Hand Signal	Tools
	None

Watch gets your dog focused on you. Once your dog has perfected it, she will be able to retain her focus even with distractions, such as treats or toys. This skill is both impressive from an obedience standpoint and useful for training. We recommend that you not use a clicker for this trick, as the clicker can draw your dog's attention away from you. Use your voice as a marker instead by praising.

1 Praise and reward when your dog makes eye contact with you. If you need to, point to your eyes to draw your dog's attention to your face.

2 Gradually extend the length of time that your dog has to maintain eye contact. Add in your verbal cue by saying "Watch me" when your dog looks at you. You should also work in a release word, such as "Okay!" or "Free" to tell your dog when she can break eye contact.

3

Add in distractions to test your dog's focus. Start by holding your hands out to either side of you, and then work up to moving your hands around and practicing in busy places.

ON THE MOVE

You can also use Watch on the move, which is great to know for walking through crowds or keeping your dog's attention on you if another dog is trying to start trouble. To teach this, tell your dog to "Watch me," and then take a step forward. Praise and reward if she maintains focus. Gradually increase the distance you can move without your dog looking away from you. This is challenging, but with practice, your dog will master it.

Front

Teaching your dog to come to your front is useful for positioning your dog for other tricks and gives her a specific place to aim for when you call her. You will be able to work up to calling your dog to Front from a distance, so that no matter where she is, she knows to come sit in front of you.

Verbal Cue	Prerequisites
"Front"	Sit
Hand Signal	Tools
None	None

USING WITH DOWN OR WHEN STANDING

Depending on what other tricks you are using Front with, you can ask your dog to do a Down or to stand in the Front position.

Use a treat or toy to lure your dog into a Sit in front of you. Praise and reward for the Sit in front.

Add in your verbal cue by saying "Front" and then luring her into position. Repeat until she is doing this consistently and starting to anticipate the lure.

Fade out the lure so your dog is coming to your front just on your verbal cue.

 ## DOG TREAT

Gradually increase the distance you can call your dog from. If your dog starts to have trouble when you increase distance, pat your legs to help her out. You can also do this to encourage her to come closer if she is sitting farther away than you want her to.

Go to My Side

Verbal Cue	Prerequisites
"Side" (optional)	Front
Hand Signal	Tools
On left (Direct Route); on right (Wrap Around)	None

Go to My Side is another trick that puts your dog in a position to then go on to a different trick. It can also come in handy if your dog tries to trip you on walks! You can send your dog to your side in two ways: going directly there and turning around or wrapping around your body. We will show you how to teach both; you can choose the version that works best for you and your dog (or do both!).

Direct Route

Start with your dog in front of you. Use a lure in your left hand to guide her to your left side. Lead her nose out from and a little behind your body, and then turn so she comes in close to your side. Reward when she is next to your left side.

Repeat luring your dog to your left side several times until your dog is easily following the lure to your left.

Gradually fade out your lure so you can just move your hand to your left to signal Go to My Side instead of luring her the whole way. Add in a verbal cue if you want to by saying "Side" and then giving your dog the hand signal.

TROUBLESHOOTING

Ideally, you want your dog to end up close to your side and facing straight ahead. Sometimes, however, your dog may position herself too far away or swing her rear out so she is crooked when asked to Sit or Down at your side. There are a few ways to fix these problems.

If your dog goes to your side but is too far away from you, try going back to the luring step to reinforce that right next to you is the best place to be. As you fade the lure, you can then make sure to only reward her when she comes in close.

Another option is to stand close to a wall, fence, or other barrier so your dog has to be right next to your side. You can then fade this barrier to something smaller, such as a tipped-over chair or flower-pot, and work toward not needing any barrier at all. This method also works well for dogs that end up crooked when asked to Sit or Down. The barrier will prevent your dog from swinging her rear out.

If she regresses at any point, just go back to work next to a wall a few times to remind her what the correct position is.

Wrap Around

Start with the lure in your right hand. Lead your dog's nose to your right, staying close to your body.

Reach behind you to switch the lure from your right hand to your left hand.

Lure your dog the rest of the way to your left side using your left hand. Reward when she is in position next to your left leg.

Repeat steps 1 through 3 until your dog is easily following the lure around your body.

GOING TO THE RIGHT

You can also teach your dog to go to your right side using either the Direct or Wrap Around methods. Just switch "left" and right" in the instructions and follow all of the steps as altered.

5

Gradually fade out your lure until you can just move your right hand to signal your dog to go around you to your left side. You can now add in a verbal cue if you want to by saying "Side" and then giving your dog the hand signal.

DOG TREAT

If you are teaching your dog multiple ways to go to one or both of your sides, either use hand signals only or use a different verbal cue for each one. As well as "Side," some other options are "Wrap," "Swing," and "Heel."

Easy Button or Service Bell

Verbal Cue	Prerequisites
"Hit it"	Targeting
Hand Signal	**Tools**
None	Easy Button or service bell

This trick, using an Easy Button or a service bell, is fun to teach. The sound that your button or bell makes acts as an additional marker that your dog has done the trick correctly! This trick can easily be shaped, or you can place a target on top of the button and phase it out. This version takes you through how to shape it.

DOG TREAT

This trick has a lot of room for creativity with your verbal cue, especially when it comes to the type of sound the button or bell makes. If using the Staples® Easy Button™, you could ask your dog "Was that hard?" For the service bell, some options are "Butler!" or "Suppertime!" There are also a wide variety of sound buttons you can find in stores and online which will allow you to use other creative phrases.

Place the Easy Button on the ground and click and reward when your dog looks at it.

Click and reward when your dog touches the button with either her nose or her paw. Repeat two or three times to make sure she understands.

A paw works best for this trick, so start to click only when your dog uses her paw to hit the button. At this point, she does not need to press hard enough to make noise. Repeat until she is consistently using her paw.

Hold your rewards until your dog pushes on the button hard enough to make a sound. Give her lots of praise to let her know the noise is a good thing. She will quickly figure out that the object must make the sound before she gets a reward.

Add in your verbal cue by saying "Hit it" before your dog hits the button. Only reward her if she hits the button when you have asked her to.

Lights On/ Lights Off

Verbal Cue	Prerequisites
"Lights"	Touch, Targeting
Hand Signal	Tools
	Push-button light

Turning a light on and off is a fun, useful trick for your dog to know. For this, we recommend using a push-button light that can be stuck on the wall at a height appropriate for your dog so she can easily reach it.

DOG TREAT

If your dog goes to grab the light with her teeth, just ignore her until she touches the light straight on with her nose. You can also have her do a Touch to your hand over the light to remind her what motion you are looking for.

1 Apply the light to a wall where it will be used and hold your hand over the light as if signaling your dog to Touch. Click and reward when your dog touches your hand with her nose. Repeat one or two times until she understands.

2 Start to fade out the use of your hand by spreading your hand around the light. Click and reward when your dog touches the actual light. Repeat until she is consistently touching the light.

3

Now only touch the top of the light with a finger to guide your dog, and click and reward when she presses on the light with her nose. Repeat until she is doing this consistently.

4

Remove your hand entirely, and click and reward when your dog touches the light without assistance. You can now add in your verbal cue by saying "Lights" before she presses the light. Work up to sending her to the light from across the room.

USING A PAW

If your dog likes to use her paws, you can teach her to use a paw to press the light. That said, be aware of your dog's enthusiasm level and how much force she uses. If your dog tends to get excited and slam things with her paws (like our model), we recommend you discourage her from using her paw for this trick so she doesn't damage your house.

Cross Paws

Verbal Cue	Prerequisites
"Crisscross"	Down, Targeting
Hand Signal	Tools
None	Target

We all love when our dogs cross their paws on their own—it looks like they're posing! For this trick, your dog will need to hit the target with her paw, not her nose, so review that separately if she's a little rusty.

CLEVER CUES

This trick can fit a number of clever verbal cues. Some other examples are "Almost done!" or "Five more minutes?" implying that your dog is waiting on you. Play with tone so your dog will know when you are using the phrase as a command. You can also experiment with crossing your arms as a hand signal so your dog is mimicking you. Use your imagination!

Put your dog in a Down position and place the target on one of her paws. You may want to experiment to see which paw your dog prefers to have on top.

Tell your dog to touch the target. If she uses her nose, ignore the behavior. When she tries with her paw, click and reward with praise and a treat.

Shift the target so that your dog will have to reach a little more and actually cross her paws to hit it, repeating several times to build up muscle memory. Add in your verbal cue when your dog reliably crosses her paws by saying "Crisscross" before she does it.

Fade the target until she is crossing her paws without it and just use the verbal cue.

DOG TREAT

If your dog knocks the target out of place but her paw lands in the correct place, click and reward. You can then put the target back before continuing.

Shy

Verbal Cue	Prerequisites
"Are you shy?"	None
Hand Signal	**Tools**
None	None

Shy is similar to Salute but requires your dog to keep her paw on her muzzle for several seconds. This trick is great for dogs who like to use their paws, and can make for a fun conversation starter.

DOING THE TRICK FROM A DOWN

For dogs who have trouble with balance or coordination, you can also teach this trick with them in a Down. First, click and reward when your dog puts her head on the ground. You can then work toward getting her to put her paw over her face.

Click and reward when your dog raises her paw. Repeat until she is lifting her paw fairly high.

Wait until her paw makes contact with her face to click and reward. Repeat until she is consistently touching her face with her paw.

3

Require your dog to touch the top of her muzzle with her paw before you click and reward; to do this, she needs to duck her head. Repeat until she is doing this consistently.

DOG TREAT

If your dog isn't getting her paw anywhere near her face, you can put a small piece of Scotch or masking tape on her muzzle, and then click and reward when she swipes it off with her paw. You can then gradually fade the use of the tape until she puts her paw on her nose without it.

4

Add in your verbal cue by saying "Are you shy?" before she puts her paw on her nose. Gradually increase the length of time she holds the position.

Gimme a Kiss

Verbal Cue	Prerequisites
"Gimme a kiss"	None
Hand Signal	Tools
	Peanut butter

Giving a kiss can be a sweet and simple trick that is popular with a crowd. Some dogs love to dole out sloppy kisses, while others are shyer and may take some persuading—either way, this trick is sure to be a charmer.

PET PAUSE

This is not a good trick for a wild or rambunctious dog, because she could accidentally hurt someone if she's too forceful. However, no matter what your dog's disposition is, always ask any people involved if they want a kiss before letting your dog deliver one. Some people have health issues or simply feel nervous about a dog's face being close to their own.

Start by getting your dog's attention on your face. Point to the side of your face as the signal; most dogs will immediately look at your face. Reward for the look—use verbal praise first, but add in a click and treat if your dog seems reluctant.

Click and treat if your dog moves her nose toward your face.

Wait until your dog actually touches your face to click and treat again. If this is all you want your dog to do, you can add in your verbal cue now by saying "Gimme a kiss" and then rewarding when your dog complies.

If you want your dog to actually lick your cheek, try waiting for her to do it on her own. You can put a dab of peanut butter or liverwurst on your cheek to tempt her, if necessary. Once she licks, add in your verbal cue by saying "Gimme a kiss" before she licks.

If you used the peanut butter or liverwurst as a lure, fade it until your dog is kissing your plain cheek. Don't forget to praise and reward!

Tell Me a Secret

Verbal Cue	Prerequisites
"Tell me a secret"	None
Hand Signal	Tools
	Peanut butter

Tell Me a Secret is similar to Gimme a Kiss but requires your dog to specifically snuffle or lick your ear. Due to this specificity, we recommend using peanut butter or some other treat to draw your dog's attention to your ear. Warning: the early stages of training this trick can be a little messy!

! PET PAUSE

If you have ear piercings, consider what type of earrings you have on before doing this trick. Hoops or other large, dangly earrings can easily get caught in your dog's mouth. For the early steps with peanut butter, we recommend removing earrings entirely.

Also, for those with long hair, clip or tie your hair back to keep it free from peanut butter.

Put a small dab of peanut butter on your ear and encourage your dog to lick it. You may need to point to your face to show her where the peanut butter is. Click and praise when she touches your ear.

Dab some more peanut butter on your ear, and repeat letting her lick it off until she is going toward your ear without extra guidance. Always praise when she licks or touches your ear.

3

Add in your verbal cue by saying "Tell me a secret" before letting your dog lick the peanut butter from your ear.

4

Fade the use of peanut butter by using less and less until your dog touches your ear on command without any peanut butter present. Click and reward each time with a separate treat now that she doesn't have the automatic reward of the peanut butter.

DOG TREAT

For dogs that don't like or can't have peanut butter due to allergy or dietary restrictions, any soft, spreadable treat will work for this trick. Some other options are liverwurst, squeezable cheese, liver paste in a can, almond butter, canned pumpkin, or apple butter.

Spin

Verbal Cue	Prerequisites
"Spin"	None

Hand Signal	Tools
	None

Spin is a complete counterclockwise turn, which can be done with your dog next to or in front of you (or at a distance!). Just like how most people are left- or right-handed, many dogs are "pawed"—they can naturally turn in one direction more easily and comfortably than the other. This makes Spin a nice companion trick to teach with Twirl (which goes the other direction).

! PET PAUSE

This is not an ideal trick for elderly dogs, young puppies, or dogs with back problems. Be mindful of your dog's physical abilities, and don't ask her to turn too tightly.

Use a treat or toy to lure your dog's head back toward her tail. This is easiest to do with your left hand, which will eventually become your hand signal. Reward for any motion in the correct direction (counterclockwise, or to your dog's left).

Still luring, have your dog make a full circle before rewarding. Add in your verbal cue by telling her to "Spin" before you start to lure.

Fade the lure. Your dog will start to anticipate the turn on her own when she hears the word "Spin," and you will be able to get your hand signal down to a movement of your hand or a flick of your fingers. At this point, you can also fade out the use of the treat in your hand.

DOG TREAT

This trick is a great place to use body language to help your dog. As you fade the lure so you are no longer making the full circle with your hand, try leaning your body as an extra cue. Because your dog is supposed to turn to her left and is looking at you, you will need to lean to your right. If she is making eye contact as she tries to remember what she's supposed to do, her head will follow yours, causing her to lean in the correct direction. This can be all the extra help your dog needs!

Twirl

Verbal Cue	Prerequisites
"Twirl"	None
Hand Signal	Tools
	None

Twirl is a complete clockwise turn, or the opposite of Spin. Teaching your dog this in combination with Spin is a good way to ensure balanced use of her muscles. Twirl can be done with your dog in front of you, next to you, or at a distance once she has connected the turn with the verbal cue.

! PET PAUSE

As with Spin, this trick is not ideal for dogs who have back problems or delicate joints (think young and elderly dogs). Use discretion, and don't ask your dog to turn more tightly than she can do comfortably.

1

Use a treat or toy to lure your dog's head to her right. This is easiest to do with your right hand, which will eventually be used for your hand signal. Reward for any movement of her body.

2

Lure your dog in a complete clockwise circle and reward. Add in your verbal cue by telling her to "Twirl" before you start to lure.

3

Fade the lure. Adding a slight pause between giving the verbal cue and luring gives your dog a chance to interpret the command and anticipate the lure, so she will at least start to turn on the verbal cue alone. You can work down to just needing a slight motion of your hand to signal Twirl.

DISTANCE WORK

Once your dog has mastered the verbal cue for Twirl, you can add distance. An easy way to get your dog away from you is to send her to a target and then tell her to Twirl. If she comes back to you, just send her out again. If she looks confused, try giving your hand signal or leaning to your left (her right) to help her out. When rewarding for a job well done, toss the treat to your dog or behind her to reinforce staying out by the target instead of coming back in to you.

Jump Over My Legs

Verbal Cue	Prerequisites
"Over"	None
Hand Signal	Tools
	None

Most dogs love to jump and leap. This trick teaches your dog to jump on cue. Do not try this until your dog is old enough to jump, and avoid this trick with large dogs who might accidentally injure you if they slip while jumping.

TARGET METHOD

You can also teach this trick using a target. Place the target on the opposite side of your legs from your dog, and then tell her to go to it. You can then gradually fade out the target and add in your verbal cue as in steps 3 and 4.

Sit on the ground with your legs out straight in front of you.

Use a lure to get your dog to step or hop over your legs. Praise and reward when your dog completes the jump. Repeat several times until your dog is comfortable hopping over your legs.

3

Add in your verbal cue by saying "Over" before starting to lure your dog over your legs. She will quickly start to anticipate the jump when she hears your command.

DOG TREAT

Depending on the physical abilities of both you and your dog, you may be able to work up to asking your dog to jump over your outstretched leg while standing up (or, for a smaller dog, kneeling).

4

Gradually fade the lure until your dog only needs a small signal or jumps over your legs just on your command.

Jump Through a Hoop

Verbal Cue	Prerequisites
"Hoop"	None
Hand Signal	Tools
	Hula hoop

Circus-type tricks are always fun, and Jump Through a Hoop is no exception. Choose a hoop that is big enough for your dog to easily jump through, and start off with one that doesn't make any noise when shaken.

! PET PAUSE

Raise the hoop only as high as your dog can jump through safely. Be mindful of her age and build when determining how high she can jump, and when in doubt, err toward having her jump lower.

Stand the hoop up on the ground and lure your dog toward it. You can either hold the hoop yourself or ask a friend to help out.

Repeat luring your dog through the hoop several times until your dog is going through it with minimal help. Always reward when she hops all the way through.

3

Add in the verbal cue "Hoop" when your dog reliably goes through the hoop. Fade the lure until your dog steps through the hoop when she hears your verbal cue. You can then gradually try raising the hoop a few inches at a time according to your dog's physical abilities.

RING OF FIRE

To add some extra flair to your hula hoop, tape red, orange, and/or yellow crepe paper to the top of it. You now have a "ring of fire" for your dog to jump through! She may be wary of the flapping paper at first, so go back to step 1 to show her that this is just like jumping through a regular hoop.

Sit Pretty

Verbal Cue	Prerequisites
"Pretty!"	Sit
Hand Signal	**Tools**
None	None

Sit Pretty (also known as Sit Up or Beg) is a classic trick that everyone knows and loves. It is great for taking cute photos of your dog and can also be paired with other tricks, such as Wave, Salute, or Treat on Your Nose.

! PET PAUSE

This trick requires good balance and puts a strain on your dog's back, so it is not a good choice for dogs with back problems or arthritis. Even if you have a young dog, only ask her to Sit Pretty a few times a day so she doesn't wear herself out. Done with fit young dogs, this trick will improve balance and build core muscle strength.

Start with your dog in a Sit.

Using a treat or toy as a lure, lead your dog's nose up and a little bit back so she leans onto her hind quarters and raises her front feet off the ground. Praise and reward when she is sitting up. Repeat until she is doing this easily.

3

Add in your verbal cue by saying "Pretty!" and then using the lure.

DOG TREAT

Some other verbal cue options we have heard for this trick are "Beg" and "Gopher." "Gopher" is especially perfect if you have a small dog!

You can also choose to use a hand signal for this trick, such as a thumbs-up sign. To do this, start giving your hand signal either before luring or as you lure once your dog is readily sitting up. You can then either always give the signal above your dog's head or gradually work toward having your hand closer to your body.

4

Fade the lure until your dog will sit up on just the verbal cue. If she needs a little help, feel free to move your hand as if you still had the lure as a reminder.

Head Tilt

Verbal Cue	Prerequisites
"Dinner?"	None
Hand Signal	**Tools**
None	None

Many dogs tilt their heads when they hear a strange noise or a word they understand. For some dogs, the tilt is subtle, while others look like their heads are about to fall off their shoulders! The trick (pun intended) to training this trick is to catch your dog tilting her head.

DOG TREAT

If your dog becomes desensitized to the magic word or sound during training and stops tilting her head, take a break and come back to this trick later. Head tilting is a reflex behavior that your dog is doing unconsciously, so it may take several training sessions for her to figure out what you are clicking for. Once she does, finalizing the verbal cue will go quickly.

Get your dog's attention, and make note of what her natural, relaxed head position is.

Say a word or make a noise that causes your dog to tilt her head. Click and reward for even a small tilt. Repeat until she is consistently tipping her head.

Fade out any other words or noises by giving your verbal cue "Dinner?" and then following it with a chirp. Repeat until your dog anticipates the chirp and tilts her head on the verbal cue alone.

CHANGING THE VERBAL CUE

Your dog may automatically tilt her head if you say a word that she knows and likes, such as "squirrel" or "cookies." If that is the case, you can easily use that word as your verbal cue for this trick, or you can go through the process of transferring the head-tilt reaction to a different word or phrase as in step 3.

You can also use a question as your verbal cue, such as "Are you confused?," "Where's daddy?," or "Want a pony?"

Nod Yes

Verbal Cue	Prerequisites
"Do you like …?"	Sit, Wait
Hand Signal	Tools
None	None

For this trick, your verbal cue will become a question your dog answers by nodding yes. Moving her head in a bobbing motion up and down is not a natural movement for your dog, so we recommend you teach this trick using luring instead of shaping. You can use treats or a toy depending on what your dog finds to be the most rewarding.

! PET PAUSE

At first, your dog may try to jump up and steal the lure while working on this trick. If she does, just put her back into position and try again. You may also need to do a quick review of the command Wait.

Tell your dog to Sit and Wait, and then get her attention with a treat or toy.

Move the lure so her head drops into a nod and then comes back up to level. Repeat several times to get her accustomed to the movement.

Add in your verbal cue by saying "Do you like ...?" before luring. Repeat until she starts to anticipate the lure and nod on her own.

GOING BEYOND "DO YOU LIKE"

This trick is very versatile, allowing you to have some fun with it. Because your verbal cue is the partial question "Do you like ...?" you can add anything to finish the sentence. This could be "Do you like biscuits?" or "Do you like the beach?" In either case, your dog will nod because she hears the phrase "Do you like ...?" Experiment with tone to clue your dog in that your question is actually the verbal cue.

You can also use different phrases for your verbal cue, such as "Nod" or "Do you want ...?" You can even teach her to nod when she hears any of those three commands.

Gradually fade the lure until your dog nods on your command without any assistance.

Shake Your Head No

Verbal Cue	Prerequisites
"Bad dog"	Sit, Wait
Hand Signal	Tools
None	None

This trick is especially popular if you are doing a school demo. Children may even offer scenarios for you to use as your question! As you teach this, know that a sideways motion of your dog's head is not a natural movement for her. For that reason, you should plan on luring this behavior instead of shaping it. You can also get your dog to shake her head by blowing on her ear, but many dogs do not appreciate that.

 DOG TREAT

Most dogs bend more easily to one side or the other. Experiment with which direction your dog prefers, and use that for this trick. You can also teach her to do a complete head shake in both directions.

Tell your dog to Sit and Wait, and then get her attention with a lure.

Lure her head to the side and then back. Repeat several times until she is easily following the motion and starts to anticipate your lure.

3

Add in your verbal cue by saying "Bad dog" in a neutral voice before starting the lure.

FUN WITH VERBAL CUES

Once your dog has mastered this trick, you can ask her "Are you a bad dog?" and she will shake her head to say "No!" Use a neutral or playful tone of voice so your dog distinguishes between this trick and when she is actually in trouble.

You can also use a different word or phrase as your verbal cue to work into a question. For example, you can use "Hate" as your verbal cue, and then ask your dog "Do you hate going to bed early?" If you consistently put the emphasis on the word "hate," you can then do a number of questions that include "hate" as her cue.

4

Gradually fade the lure until your dog shakes her head on just your verbal cue.

Look Up

Verbal Cue	Prerequisites
"Look up"	Sit, Wait
Hand Signal	**Tools**
	None

You can use this trick to draw your dog's attention to something above her, or to distract her from something that she is afraid of on the ground. Looking up is easy to teach through shaping if your dog naturally looks at the sky, but most dogs tend to keep their focus on the ground. For these dogs, luring is a quicker method to teach Look Up.

DOG TREAT

Some dogs will pick up this trick just from you pointing up without a lure. Another way to help fade your lure is to practice under a tree, inside your house, or any other location where your dog might have a reason to look up on her own. You can then praise and reward when she does.

Tell your dog to Sit and Wait, and then get her attention with a lure.

Raise the lure over your dog's head so she looks up toward the sky. Reward when her head is pointing upward. Repeat until she is easily tilting her head back without jumping up.

Add in your verbal cue by saying "Look up" before starting the lure.

OTHER WAYS TO CUE

Be creative and have fun with whatever cue you choose. When practicing in a public place such as a park, you may find that nearby people hear your verbal cue or see your dog looking up and also look up to see what she is looking at! Some fun options for verbal cues are "Superman," "Where's the bird?," and "It's gonna crash!"

Gradually fade the lure so you can point at the sky and give your dog the verbal cue.

Poke

Verbal Cue	Prerequisites
"Go poke"	Targeting
Hand Signal	Tools
	Target

Poke is a great trick to use when there are other people around or to get someone's attention. Dogs that like to use their nose and enjoy socializing will especially love this trick. For the training process, you will need a friend to help you a little as the one your dog goes to.

IF YOU DON'T HAVE A HELPER

If you don't have a helper most of the time, you can start teaching this trick by holding the target against your own leg and working through all of the steps. Then, when you do have a friend to help out, your dog will already know the foundation, and you can quickly teach her to do the same thing to another person.

1

Have your helper hold a target against her leg where your dog can easily reach it. Click and reward when your dog looks at the target.

2

Click and reward when your dog touches the target. If needed, give your Targeting command as a reminder. Repeat until she is consistently going to the target and touching it with her nose.

Add in your verbal cue by saying "Go poke" before you send your dog to the target.

Gradually fade the target by using a smaller target (stickers also work well for this). As the target gets smaller, your helper can point to her leg to give your dog an extra hint.

Phase out the use of your helper's hand so your dog goes and touches her leg without any help.

Bow

Verbal Cue	Prerequisites
"Ta-da!"	None
Hand Signal	Tools
None	None

Bow is the perfect way to end a trick performance and can also be a fun way to have your dog greet or say good-bye to people. Bow can be combined with Wag Your Tail for a very positive greeting.

! PET PAUSE

This trick may be difficult for some older dogs that have arthritis. If your dog seems to be uncomfortable when trying to Bow or acts sore after a training session, think about trying a different trick instead.

You may also find that your dog goes into a stretch after she initially bows. To stop that behavior, only reward when she is in a stationary Bow position. You can also teach her Stretch as a separate trick!

Use a treat or toy to lure your dog's nose down and back between her front paws so she drops her front end. If she doesn't keep her rear end up on her own, use a hand under her to gently prop her up.

Fade out your support hand until your dog bows without the hand holding her up.

Add in your verbal cue by saying "Ta-da!" before you lure her into Bow.

DOG TREAT

We use "Ta-da!" as the verbal cue for Bow because "Bow" and "Down" sound so similar and can be confusing for the dog. Another way to deal with this issue is to train your dog to do Bow by bowing yourself as you give your verbal cue. This combination of signal and verbal cue makes it clear to your dog which trick you want her to do, because you will never bow when asking her to Down.

Fade the lure so your dog does Bow on your verbal cue alone.

Wag Your Tail

Wag Your Tail is an easy trick to train because all dogs wag their tails! Once your dog wags her tail on command, you can combine your verbal cue with other phrases, such as "If you want a biscuit, wag your tail!"

Verbal Cue	Prerequisites
"Wag your tail"	Front
Hand Signal	Tools
None	None

DOG TREAT

When giving your verbal cue, use a happy, upbeat tone of voice. This tone will act both as an extra signal to your dog of what you want her to do and also make her happy and more likely to wag her tail. After all, dogs love when we are happy with them.

Have your dog stand in front of you and talk to her in a silly voice.

Click and reward when she wags her tail. Repeat until she starts to figure out the tail wag is what you are clicking for. You can add in your verbal cue by saying "Wag your tail."

3

Work toward getting the wag on just your verbal cue without the extra talking.

ISOLATING THE CUE

A tail wag is a reflexive action for your dog, so it may take a few sessions before she figures out what she is doing that causes you to click. Keep practicing, and she will figure it out. This trick is one of the few where you add in the verbal cue before the dog fully understands the trick. This works because even before your dog connects the cue with wagging her tail, she will connect the cue with rewards, which of course will make her wag her tail!

Go to Bed

Verbal Cue	Prerequisites
"Go to bed"	Down
Hand Signal	**Tools**
	Dog bed

This trick is both cute and practical. You can send your dog to bed as part of a skit or use it to keep her out of the way during meals. And of course it will always be applicable at bedtime!

DOG TREAT

If you want your dog to stay on the bed for a little while, review the skill Wait and remind her to do that when she settles on the bed.

Place a dog bed on the ground near your dog. Click and reward when she looks at it.

Click and reward when your dog approaches the bed. If she needs some help, feel free to point at the bed to get her interested.

Wait until your dog gets on or in the bed to click and reward. Repeat until she is consistently going to the bed.

Tell your dog to Down on the bed. At this point, only reward if she lies down on the bed. Repeat until she is doing this consistently.

Add in your verbal cue by saying "Go to bed" and then rewarding when she lies down on her bed. You can work on increasing the distance that you send her to her bed.

Go to Jail

Verbal Cue	Prerequisites
"Jail"	None
Hand Signal	**Tools**
	Dog crate

Go to Jail is an amusing way to send your dog to her crate. A really easy way to make your dog love this trick is to practice it at mealtimes by sending her to her crate to get fed!

Click and reward when your dog looks at her crate.

Click and reward when your dog approaches and/or touches the crate. Repeat a few times until she understands.

Wait until she puts her head into the crate to click and reward. Repeat a few times until she is consistently sticking her head into the crate every time she approaches it.

Now wait until your dog steps into the crate with one or two feet to click and reward. Repeat a few times. If your dog is hesitant to enter the crate, toss a few treats inside it to encourage her.

Click and reward when your dog completely gets into the crate. Add in your verbal cue by saying "Jail" or "Go to jail" and then sending her to her crate. Repeat until she is consistently going into the crate. Gradually increase the distance that you send her from.

Sit in a Chair

Many dogs love to sit in chairs. Teaching your dog to do this on command can be fun for both of you and give you a perfect place to have your dog stay while next to you at a picnic or outdoor event.

Verbal Cue	Prerequisites
"Hop in the chair!"	Sit
Hand Signal	**Tools**
None	Chair

1

Click and reward when your dog looks at the chair.

2

Click and reward when your dog approaches the chair.

3

Click and reward when your dog touches the chair. For the moment, it does not matter if she uses her nose or paw. Repeat a few times until she understands.

4

Wait for her to touch the chair with her paw. Repeat several times until she is consistently touching the chair with her paw. If she is having trouble, you can use a target to help her out.

5

Click and reward when she puts her paw on top of the seat of the chair. At this point, only reward if her paw is on top of the chair. Repeat until she is doing this consistently.

PET PAUSE

You should choose a sturdy chair that won't tip when your dog climbs on it. Avoid slippery metal chairs or ones with woven straps on the seat, as a paw could get caught between the straps. If your dog is uncomfortable with an open-backed chair, find one that has solid material.

6

7

Click and reward when your dog puts two feet on top of the chair. Repeat several times.

Wait until your dog completely hops into the chair to click and reward, giving her encouragement if she needs it. Add in your verbal cue by saying "Hop in the chair!" before sending her to it. Repeat until she is reliably getting into the chair on her own.

LURING METHOD

You can also teach this trick by luring your dog up and into the chair.

Add a Sit when she is in the chair.

 DOG TREAT

If you want your dog to remain in the chair for a little while, review your Wait command and tell her to wait once she has settled into the chair. Just be sure to never leave your dog unattended in a public place.

Get in a Box

Verbal Cue	Prerequisites
"Load up!"	Sit, Down
Hand Signal	**Tools**
None	Box

While dogs aren't quite as crazy about boxes as cats are, they are curious and enjoy tucking themselves in once they learn this trick. Make sure your box is both easy for your dog to step into and big enough for her to fit!

Put your box on the ground and encourage your dog to approach. Click and reward for the approach. When rewarding, toss the treat a little away from the box so your dog will have to make an effort to come back to it.

Click and reward if your dog touches the box at all.

Now click and reward only if your dog touches the box with a paw.

Wait for your dog to put her paw into the box. Click and reward. Give her the treat while her paw is still in the box to reinforce that position.

Once she is putting one paw in the box regularly, raise the stakes and require two paws. You can praise her for putting one paw in the box, but don't click and reward until she puts two paws in.

DOG TREAT

There are many fun commands you can use for this trick. Some other examples are the following:

"Mail-order doggy!"

"Hide!"

"Express shipment!"

"Gift box!"

"Return to sender!"

6

While your dog may just skip to putting all four paws in, click and reward if she puts three paws in. In either case, let her know how brilliant she is!

LURING METHOD

If your dog does not seem to understand the shaping process for Get in a Box, you can easily teach this trick with luring. Use treats to get her to approach the box and step in. Be sure to praise and treat when she gets any paw in the box. You can then raise the criteria to gradually increase the number of feet in the box. Once she is getting into the box willingly, add in your verbal cue before luring and then gradually fade out your lure until she will get into the box on just your command.

7

Wait for her to put all four feet in the box to click and reward. Once she is reliably putting all four feet in the box, you can add your verbal cue by saying "Load up!" before letting her go to the box.

DOG TREAT

Once your dog has mastered getting into the box, you can ask her to Sit or Down in the box. You can also try getting her to do other tricks if they fit!

Pee on Command

Verbal Cue	Prerequisites
"Hurry"	None
Hand Signal	**Tools**
None	None

Although this isn't your typical trick, Pee on Command is great for when you need to get going somewhere but know your dog needs to pee. This is also helpful when traveling with your dog when you want to be sure she eliminates in a suitable place.

CLEVER CUES

We like "Hurry" for when it is raining or snowing outside, but there are many other common commands for telling a dog to pee. Some of the most common are "Do your business," "Potty," and "Go pee."

Wait until a time when you usually take your dog outside and take her to a place where she likes to pee. Give your verbal cue by saying "Hurry" and then praising when she pees.

Reward for a job well done! Your dog might think you're a little crazy, but a treat easily earned is still a treat.

3

Repeat every time you know your dog needs to pee. She will connect your command with peeing, and eventually you will be able to tell her to pee.

DOG TREAT

This is a great behavior to combine with housebreaking a new puppy. Every time you take your puppy outside (which will be a lot), tell her to "Hurry" and then praise and reward when she pees outside. This both teaches her your verbal cue and also reinforces peeing outside rather than in the house.

It is equally easy and effective to teach an adult dog who is new to your family, whether she is a shelter adoptee or a rescue dog. Some older dogs that are being rehomed may already know to Pee on Command, so you can use that to tell her where on your property it is okay to pee.

Scratch Board

Verbal Cue	Prerequisites
"Scratch"	Targeting
Hand Signal	**Tools**
None	Scratch board

This trick is both cute and files down the nails of dogs who hate having their nails cut. All you need to get started is a board and some sandpaper or stair tread.

MAKING IT EASIER

For older dogs or dogs that have back problems or balance issues, this trick can be taught with the scratch board flat on the ground.

Lean your scratch board against a wall or ask a friend to support it so it stays steady. Click and reward when your dog looks at the board.

Click and reward when your dog touches the board. For the moment, she can use either her nose or paw. You can hold a target against the board to help her out if needed.

Start to reward only when your dog uses her paw to touch the board. Repeat until she is doing this consistently.

DOG TREAT

The ideal form for scratching is for your dog to stand at an angle to the board and scratch with her outside paw, or the one farthest from the board. This allows the nails to be filed down evenly. You can then reorient your dog to the other side of the board to scratch with her other paw. Always check your dog's pads afterward to make sure they haven't accidentally been rubbed raw.

Wait for your dog to scratch at the board before you click and reward. Work up to a more intense scratch, with your dog using both of her paws. You can now add in your verbal cue by saying "Scratch" before she goes to the board.

PART 3:
Intermediate
Tricks

Stretch

Verbal Cue	Prerequisites
"Stretch"	None
Hand Signal	Tools
None	None

All dogs stretch. The challenge with this trick is getting your dog to stretch on command, rather than just when he feels like it. We'll give you some tips on how to do that.

USING BODY LANGUAGE

You can also teach your dog to stretch when you stretch yourself. When working on step 2, stretch at the same time as or instead of giving your verbal cue. Some dogs already stretch with their owners every morning by coincidence, making this an easy signal to train.

Click and reward whenever your dog stretches. Repeat until he starts to stretch around you on purpose (even just a partial stretch) or to come to you when he needs to stretch.

Add in your verbal cue by saying "Stretch" before or as your dog stretches.

Work up to an on-demand stretch, at which point your dog will stretch when he hears your verbal cue.

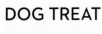

DOG TREAT

The biggest challenge with this trick is getting your dog to stretch in the first place so you can click and reward. Before you start training, spend a few days paying attention to your dog's routine and when he normally stretches. Most dogs stretch when they get up from a nap, and others stretch if they have been in a crate for a while and are let out. Use this information to your advantage.

If your dog stretches after sleeping, have your clicker ready by your bed in the morning so you can click and reward when he wakes up. During the day, watch for him to get up from a nap to click and reward for that stretch as well.

If your dog stretches when he comes out of his crate, put him in his crate for a little bit while you do something else. You can then have your clicker ready when you let him out. This also works well if your dog is crated while you are away at work or school, because you can reward him for stretching when you get home.

Get Your Bowl

Verbal Cue	Prerequisites
"Dinnertime"	Fetch, Drop It or Give
Hand Signal	Tools
None	Bowl

Your dog can help with chores at home by learning how to fetch his dinner bowl! Choose a bowl that is safe and easy for your dog to carry, such as stainless steel with a lip.

Place the bowl on the ground. Click and reward when your dog looks at it. If necessary, help him by pointing.

Click and reward when your dog approaches the bowl.

Reward for touching the bowl with his nose. If he goes to paw at the bowl, just ignore that action.

Wait for your dog to grab the bowl. If you are using a solid bowl, you will be able to hear his teeth click on it. Click and reward!

Wait for your dog to lift the bowl. At first, reward him for lifting it even a tiny bit. You can then gradually require him to fully pick it up.

PET PAUSE

For your dog's water bowl, we recommend using a different and possibly heavier bowl to prevent him from grabbing the wrong one and spilling it. Another option is to get a bucket you can clip to his crate so he can't move it.

Place the bowl a little away from you and encourage him to bring it to you. Feel free to use your Fetch command to help him understand what you want him to do. Use Drop It or Give when he brings the bowl to you.

Switch to your "Dinnertime" verbal cue to tell your dog that you don't want him to fetch just anything—you want him to specifically get his bowl.

DOG TREAT

If your dog is uncomfortable carrying metal, you can use a different type of bowl instead. Try a plastic or light ceramic bowl, or check out collapsible bowls made of plastic or canvas.

Gradually increase the distance until you can send your dog into another room to get the bowl. Now he can bring his bowl from anywhere when it's time for dinner!

HAVE MULTIPLE DOGS?

You can still use this trick if you have multiple dogs. Either get bowls that are easy to tell apart, or keep each dog's bowl in a specific location. You can then work separately with each dog to teach him to only retrieve his bowl from the place it is kept. If he brings you the wrong bowl, don't reward him, and try again.

Bring Your Leash

Verbal Cue	Prerequisites
"Get your leash"	Fetch, Hold, Carry, Give
Hand Signal	**Tools**
None	Leash

Bring Your Leash is the perfect trick for when you want to take your dog for a walk but have left the leash in the other room. Once he learns this, you can just send your dog to go grab it himself!

! PET PAUSE

Do not allow your dog to mouth or chew the leash when he brings it to you. This can turn into a bad habit that could result in your dog both destroying a leash and getting loose in a dangerous place. To avoid this, never play with the leash with your dog, and gently correct him by tapping on his muzzle if he starts to chew.

Place the leash on the ground or floor and click and reward when your dog looks at it.

Click and reward when your dog touches the leash with his nose. Repeat until he is consistently touching the leash.

Wait until your dog grabs the leash to click and reward. Repeat until he picks up the leash every time.

DOG TREAT

Once your dog has mastered picking up the leash and bringing it to you, you can increase the distance he has to go to get it. You can also ask him to get the leash off of a coffee table or counter if that is where you normally keep it. Be aware, though—grabbing something off the counter might not be a behavior you want your dog to learn!

Encourage your dog to bring the leash to you. You can now add in your verbal cue by saying "Get your leash" before you let him go get it.

Go See

Sending your dog to another person is fun and can be useful around the house. You can send your dog to find one of your children, a friend, or a significant other. Teaching this trick works best using people your dog knows and likes.

Verbal Cue	Prerequisites
"Go see ..." or "Go find ..."	Sit, Stand, Down
Hand Signal	**Tools**
	A friend

Have your dog at your side (it doesn't matter if he is in a Sit, Stand, or Down) and position your helper a short distance away. Make sure your friend has treats or a toy to reward your dog.

Click and treat if your dog looks at your friend. If he is too focused on you (not a bad thing!), feel free to point to help him out, or ask your friend to say or do something to attract his attention.

PET PAUSE

While it can be helpful in the beginning if your helper makes a big fuss to attract your dog, you will need to fade this out pretty quickly. This trick is not like a recall; instead, you will be sending your dog away from you and want him to be able to go off and locate the person on his own. It is best to instruct your helper to be calm when you send your dog and to only praise and reward when your dog gets there.

Click and reward if your dog goes to approach your friend. When rewarding, either toss the toy or treat to your dog or have your helper give the reward. This takes the focus away from you, which is what you want for this trick.

Have your helper praise and reward your dog when he gets all the way to her.

Add in your verbal cue by saying "Go see ..." or "Go find ...," along with your helper's name. The name of the person is actually the most important part of this command, because it specifies which person. Repeat this several times.

Gradually increase the distance your dog has to go to get to your helper. Eventually, you can work up to sending your dog to find your friend from another room.

COMBINING WITH OTHER TRICKS

You can combine this trick with other tricks such as Carry and Fetch, making your canine a personal delivery dog!

USING A TARGET

You can also teach this trick using a target. Have your helper hold the target and then send your dog to it. You can then fade the target and replace the command with your "Go see ..." or "Go find ..." verbal cue and your friend's name.

Once your dog is proficient at finding one person, you can go back to the beginning and teach him a different person's name. Test this out by having both people in the room and sending your dog to each in turn.

Catch a Disc

Verbal Cue	Prerequisites
"Get it!"	Fetch, Carry, Hold, Give
Hand Signal	Tools
None	Disc

Everyone who has seen top disc dogs in action is impressed by their athleticism and how much fun both the person and the dog are having. This activity, for which you can use a cloth or hard disc, can provide great exercise for both you and your dog.

PET PAUSE

Depending on your dog's physical build and his fitness, it may not be safe for him to do leaps or flying flips. Puppies in particular should never do leaping catches. Wait until your dog's growth plates have closed (12 to 18 months of age) before you attempt any leaps.

Interest your dog in the disc by waving it and doing a little bit of tugging with the disc. If he does not act interested, move it along the ground.

Hand the disc to your dog so he can get used to grabbing it.

Throw the disc long and low so your dog doesn't have to jump very high to catch it. Have your dog bring the disc back to you using Fetch and Hold or Carry.

Tell your dog to Give when he reaches you. Trade him a treat for the disc. For added control, you can add a Sit before you take it. Immediately toss the disc again so he knows the fun does not end with the retrieve.

Adjust the speed and accuracy of your throws to help your dog catch the disc more easily. Give extra praise for great catches!

Sneeze

Verbal Cue	Prerequisites
"Achoo!"	None
Hand Signal	Tools
	None

The trick to teaching your dog to do Sneeze on command is getting him to sneeze in the first place. Once your dog has learned this trick, you may find he sneezes whenever you do!

! PET PAUSE

If you are using smells to cause your dog to sneeze, be sure to avoid any chemicals that could be bad for him. Your dog's health and well-being are much more important than one trick!

1

Click and reward or praise and reward whenever your dog sneezes. At first, reward even for just a little snuffle. Repeat until he starts to snuffle or sneeze at you on purpose (or to come to you when he needs to sneeze).

2

Add in your hand signal and verbal cue. Getting the timing right can be tricky on this. Try to anticipate your dog's sneezes or to give both cues—flicking your nose and saying "Achoo"—as he sneezes.

Work up to an on-demand sneeze, or getting your dog to sneeze when he sees you give your hand signal and hears "Achoo!"

DOG TREAT

Catching your dog sneezing is the hardest part of this trick. Before you start training, spend a few days paying attention to your dog's routine and times when he sneezes naturally. Some dogs sneeze several times when they first get up in the morning, just like many humans do. Your dog may also sneeze when exposed to certain smells, such as pollen in a nearby field, pepper, or cologne or perfume. Dogs that like to curl their lips and "grin" as they play often sneeze after having their nose wrinkled up for a while.

Once you have identified some times of day or smells that make your dog sneeze, you can plan your training strategy. If your dog sneezes first thing in the morning, have treats ready next to your bed. If he sneezes on his walks, bring your clicker along. And if playtime makes him grin and then sneeze, what better excuse to play with your dog!

You can also sometimes make your dog sneeze by blowing gently in his face.

Grin

Verbal Cue	Prerequisites
"Grin"	None
Hand Signal	Tools
	None

Does your dog have a toothy grin? He can show off his pearly whites with this trick. Any breed of dog can do Grin, but it is easiest for dogs with tight lips. The challenge for you as a trainer is to capture that grin and put it on command. Some other fun verbal cues besides "Grin" are "Show your teeth" and "Tough dog."

PET PAUSE

A grin and a snarl are not the same thing. Even though a grinning dog is showing many or all of his teeth, the rest of his body is relaxed and calm. A dog that is snarling will be tense, with a stiff tail and hackles raised, plus a harsh glint in his eye. You should keep any Grin training happy and fun.

Click and reward when your dog grins, even if it is just a slight wrinkling of his nose. Repeat until he starts to grin on purpose.

Add in your hand signal and verbal cue of "Grin" by giving both of them as your dog grins. Repeat several times to connect the hand signal and verbal cue with the action of grinning in your dog's mind.

Work up to getting your dog to Grin on demand when he sees your hand signal and hears your verbal cue.

DOG TREAT

The most difficult part of this trick is getting your dog to grin in the first place. Spend a few days paying attention to what situations cause your dog to grin, and feel free to experiment a little. Some dogs grin when their owners come home from school or work because they are excited, and many grin when they are playing.

Once you have identified a situation in which your dog naturally grins, you can use that information for your training. Have a clicker and treats on hand when you come home to reward your dog's grin, or keep them close by when you play.

Take Off My Hat

Verbal Cue	Prerequisites
"Hats off"	Fetch, Hold, Give
Hand Signal	Tools
	Hat 

A fun way to take off your hat is to have your dog do it for you! This trick works best with shaping, though you can also guide your dog a bit to help him out.

Start with the hat on the ground. Click and reward if your dog looks at or touches it.

Shape your dog to pick up the hat by clicking and rewarding only if he uses the brim, as that is the part of the hat he will be able to reach when you're wearing it.

Toss the cap and have your dog Fetch it to build up his interest in it and to continue encouraging him to grab it.

Put on the hat and sit or kneel low enough that your dog can reach your head. Tip your head so the brim of the hat is easy for your dog to reach. Touch the brim to remind him what he's been working on.

PET PAUSE

Do not try this trick with a very excitable dog who might knock you over or get out of control when trying to grab the cap. Also, be sure never to reward your dog for removing a hat without being asked first—he could really scare someone if he unexpectedly jumps at a person's face with his mouth open!

Click and reward if your dog touches the hat at all.

Wait for your dog to actually grab the brim of the hat before rewarding.

Reward for any pressure that indicates he is trying to pull the hat off your head. Some dogs may immediately pull the hat free, while others might be unsure and need to gain some confidence.

Wait for your dog to completely remove the hat from your head. You can now add in your verbal cue by saying "Hats off" and then allowing your dog to remove your hat.

DOG TREAT

Wear a loose-fitting hat so your dog can easily get it off your head. You may also need to bend or move your head to help him out. Other hat styles can be used, but baseball caps work well due to the large brim.

After a few repetitions, review Hold and Give with your dog and reward only if he takes off the hat, holds it, and then releases it into your hands.

TROUBLESHOOTING

Some dogs have trouble switching from picking up the hat off the ground to taking it off your head. If that is the case, try putting some peanut butter or other treat directly on the brim of the hat (while on your head) to entice your dog. Be sure to praise when he reaches for the hat to let him know that it is okay to do that.

Bring Me Tissues

Verbal Cue	Prerequisites
"Tissue"	Hold, Carry, Give
Hand Signal	**Tools**
None	Tissue box

Need a tissue? Ask your dog to get it! For this trick, you will need one of the square boxes with the tissue sticking out the top. Your dog will enjoy pulling the tissues out of the box, so if he gets too excited about it, you may need to keep the box out of reach between training sessions.

DOG TREAT

For dogs that like to shred tissues, spend some time reviewing Hold separately from asking your dog to pull the tissue out of the box. If he does start to shred, stop him, remind him to Hold, and try again.

Click and reward when your dog touches the tissue box with his nose. If he uses his paw, ignore him. Repeat until he is consistently using his nose.

Click and reward only if he touches the tissue itself with his nose. Repeat until he touches the tissue every time.

Wait until your dog grabs the tissue to click and reward.

Encourage your dog to pull the tissue out of the box. With practice, he will be able to pull the whole thing out. Repeat until he can pull a tissue out consistently. You can now add in your verbal cue by saying "Tissue" before letting him go to the box.

Encourage your dog to carry the tissue and give it to you. Practice until he can be sent to the box, pull out a tissue, and deliver it!

Weave Through My Legs

Verbal Cue	Prerequisites
"Weave"	None
Hand Signal	Tools
	None

Leg weaving is a neat on-the-go trick that requires coordination and cooperation from both you and your dog. Before getting started with your dog, practice walking in slow motion with an exaggerated stride. The easiest way to teach this trick is to combine luring and shaping.

DOG TREAT

If you have a large dog, hold your leg out and arched without touching the ground to give him extra room to duck under. You can then complete your step when he is all the way through.

Start with your dog on your left side. Step forward with your right foot so there is a gap under your legs, and reach down with your right hand to lure your dog through. Reward him.

Now that your dog is on your right side, step forward with your left foot and use your left hand to lure your dog under your leg. Reward when he goes through.

Try to get several steps of continuous weaving in a row, rewarding for each step.

Fade your lure and switch over to using your clicker. Step forward and wait for your dog to go under your leg. Click and reward when he does. Continue on for a few more steps until he is going through more quickly.

Add in your verbal cue by saying "Weave" and then stepping forward.

Back Up

Verbal Cue	Prerequisites
"Back" or "Beep, beep"	None
Hand Signal	**Tools**
None	None

Having your dog back up is funny, especially if you use the verbal cue "Beep, beep." Back Up is one way to set your dog up to do another trick away from you. It can also be useful if your dog is blocking a doorway or hallway and you need to get by.

🦴 DOG TREAT

A dog who loves toys may respond best if you toss his toy behind him after he backs up. This enforces backward motion rather than your dog coming forward to you for his reward. You can also toss a treat, but make sure it's visible and easy for your dog to find.

Bend your body slightly toward your dog and click and reward for any paw movement—it doesn't matter what paw or paws he moves. If your dog prefers toys for a reward, hold the toy behind your back so it is out of sight.

Lean forward again, but this time, wait for one or more of your dog's paws to move backward. Click and reward.

Require a full step backward with all four paws. Click and reward. Repeat until he is consistently taking a step (or more!) backward.

You can now add in your verbal cue by telling your dog to "Beep, beep" and leaning forward to cue him to back up. Repeat until he starts to respond to your verbal cue alone.

Gradually increase the distance (or number of steps) your dog backs up. Ideally, your dog should move back in a straight line, but he may curve some as he learns this trick. Fade out your body bend as your dog becomes comfortable with the trick.

Crawl

Verbal Cue	Prerequisites
"Crawl"	Down
Hand Signal	Tools
	None

Crawling forward is fun for your dog and helps to strengthen his core muscles. Small dogs do this very naturally, but big dogs can, too—think of your big dog reaching under the furniture for a dropped treat. This trick is easiest to teach using luring.

DOG TREAT

Some fun alternatives to the verbal cue "Crawl" are "Commando crawl" or "Sneak."

Put your dog in a Down position.

Lure your dog forward, keeping your hand along the ground or the floor with the treat. Start out by only moving a few inches.

Gradually increase the distance that your dog crawls, only rewarding when he keeps his belly on or near the ground.

OTHER WAYS TO TEACH CRAWL

If you want to shape this trick, you can speed up the process by placing your dog next to a low piece of furniture, such as a coffee table, and then going to the other side and asking him to come toward you. You can also teach this trick by sitting on the floor and luring your dog under your bent knee. With either of these methods, you can then fade the use of the prop by using a taller table or raising your knee and leg higher. Eventually, you can work up to your dog crawling with nothing over him.

Fade the lure and incorporate your verbal cue by saying "Crawl" before giving your hand signal.

Jump Through My Arms

Verbal Cue	Prerequisites
"Hoop"	Jump Through a Hoop
Hand Signal	Tools
	None

For this trick, your dog will jump through a circle made with your arms. You can teach your dog to jump through your arms from scratch, but it is easiest if you teach Jump Through a Hoop first and then use the same verbal cue. Your dog will figure out the command means to jump through whichever circular space is presented to him.

TROUBLESHOOTING

If your dog is determined to cheat and go around your arms, practice next to a wall, fence, or large piece of furniture that will block him from going around. You can also ask a helper to lure your dog through your arms.

Place a lure on the ground (toys work best because they are easy to see) and make a circle with your arms, holding them low to the ground and in between your dog and the lure.

Encourage your dog to step through your arms to get the toy. If he tries to go around your arms, catch him and bring him back. He is only allowed to get the toy if he goes through the circle.

Repeat until he stops trying to go around your arms and hops through the circle each time to get the toy.

Add in your verbal cue by saying "Hoop" before your dog goes through your arms.

Gradually fade the lure so your dog will jump through your arms just on your command and signal.

Roll Over

Verbal Cue	Prerequisites
"Roll over"	Down
Hand Signal	Tools
	None

Roll Over is a classic dog trick that delights everyone no matter how many times they see it. Most dogs seem to enjoy it, too, and often jump up after the roll, barking. Luring is the easiest way to train this trick.

PET PAUSE

Some dogs physically have trouble rolling over. This includes dogs with prominent backbones, such as Greyhounds, and older dogs with sore backs. If your dog does not enjoy this, find another trick for him.

If your dog has trust issues, he may be hesitant to expose his belly. Start by doing some other tricks with him to build up both his confidence and the bond between the two of you. You can then proceed slowly with teaching Roll Over by only working on it a little at a time.

Have your dog lie down. Using a great treat (beyond basic dog food), lure his head back over his shoulder. Be sure to reward, as this can be a muscle stretch for some dogs.

Lure your dog's head farther back so he will naturally flop onto his side. Give him a treat at this point.

3

Continue moving the lure around and over, treating at various stages of the roll. Your dog should do a complete roll. Repeat several times until your dog starts to do the roll more easily. You can add in your verbal cue by saying "Roll over" before starting the lure.

DOG TREAT

This trick can be used for fire awareness talks to demonstrate "stop, drop, and roll." A Dalmatian is the perfect dog for something like this, but other breeds and mixes are just as effective at getting this idea across to schoolchildren.

4

Gradually fade out the lure, using just your hand signal and/or verbal cue.

Jump Into My Arms

Verbal Cue	Prerequisites
"Up"	Touch
Hand Signal	Tools
	None

For this trick, your dog will learn to jump up into your arms. This trick is best for small, athletic dogs who can jump well and are easy to catch. If you have a large dog, we recommend you only teach him to hop up into your lap!

Sit on a chair or bench and tell your dog to Touch, holding your hand so he has to jump into your lap to do so. Repeat two or three times to get him used to jumping into your lap, always rewarding when he has completed the jump.

Give your hand signal and verbal cue of "Up" before you ask your dog to hop up. Repeat until he starts to anticipate and jump up into your lap without the Touch signal.

Lean against a wall or furniture, so you are not sitting but your legs are not vertical, and give the hand signal and verbal cue. You need to catch hold of your dog to prevent him from falling back down. Repeat until he is consistently making the higher jump.

USING TEAMWORK

Depending on your dog's age, size, and athleticism, you may need to bend a little to catch him when he jumps. The catch part of this trick is all about teamwork—your dog jumping up to your arms, and you helping by bringing your arms closer. With practice, you will figure out the perfect formula for a clean catch.

Stand up straight and give your dog the hand signal and verbal cue. When he jumps up, catch him and reward!

Stand on Your Hind Legs

Verbal Cue	Prerequisites
"Tall"	None
Hand Signal	**Tools**
	None

Stand on Your Hind Legs requires your dog to have good balance and coordination. This is not a good trick for dogs with back problems, but it can be a lot of fun with young, fit dogs. Luring is the simplest way to teach this trick.

Using a treat or toy, lure your dog's nose up and back so he stands up on his hind legs. Reward when he is standing up.

Continue to lure until your dog is standing up on his hind legs more easily and with less assistance. You can now add in your verbal cue by saying "Tall" before you start the lure.

3

Fade the lure so it turns into your hand signal. Lure less and less, until you can just hold your hand out and tell your dog to stand up. You can also stop using a treat or toy in your hand.

PET PAUSE

Always practice this trick on solid footing, such as grass or carpeting. Never practice on a slick surface where your dog might slip, such as tile or hardwood floors. If your house isn't carpeted, buy a small rug that is big enough for your dog and has a rubber underside that won't slide on the floor.

DOG TREAT

Some dogs may try to jump and grab at your hand to steal the lure. To stop this behavior, only reward when your dog is standing with both hind feet on the ground. This also promotes safety and balance for your dog. Another option is to use a lure that he is not as excited about, such as bland biscuits or a toy he doesn't like to play with very often.

If you taught your dog to jump up to your hand for the trick Touch, he may jump because he thinks that is what you want him to do. To eliminate this confusion, use a different hand signal that is less similar to the Touch signal, such as a closed fist or a peace sign.

Side Pass

Verbal Cue	Prerequisites
None	Front
Hand Signal	Tools
	None

A Side Pass is when your dog takes a step directly to the side, without moving forward or backward. The matching sideways movement of this trick makes it looks like you are dancing with your dog. If you teach your dog to Side Pass at your side, it can also be useful for detouring around potholes or other obstacles.

DOG TREAT

You can teach your dog to do Side Pass in both directions to encourage balanced muscle use. To do so, use your body to lean in the direction you want to go to clue in your dog on which way he needs to step. You may find that he has more trouble going in one direction than the other. Give him extra help with his harder side until he has mastered the footwork.

Starting with your dog standing in front of you, take a small step to the side. Click and reward when your dog moves sideways to follow you. If he only moves his front end and is crooked, straighten him out by telling him to Front and then try again.

Work up to taking a full sideways step with your dog stepping with you. If needed, hold out one of your legs to act as a guide to keep your dog's body straight.

Fade the use of your leg so your dog will step sideways just by following your sideways motion. Ideally, he will cross his legs as he steps. Pointing with both hands works as a good hand signal because it creates a sort of channel for your dog to aim for; when the hands move sideways as you step, they are an additional signal that your dog should also move.

SIDE PASS FROM YOUR SIDE

You can also teach this trick with your dog standing at your side. If you are stepping toward your dog, use a lure in your hand to keep his head straight and prevent him from wrapping around your front, like in the photos. If you are stepping away from your dog, try patting your leg to get him to come with you. Only reward if he isn't crooked.

Close the Drawer

Verbal Cue	Prerequisites
"Close it"	None
Hand Signal	**Tools**
None	Set of drawers

Using household chores as tricks is a great way to incorporate training your dog into day-to-day life. For this trick, find a set of drawers that opens and closes easily and is an appropriate size for your dog. Don't count on your dog to close a drawer with treats or toys in it, though!

TAKING IT FURTHER

Look for a small, easy-to-transport chest of drawers to use for this trick. Garage sales and secondhand stores are excellent places to look. The drawers that we used were intended to hold jewelry and are the perfect size for a small dog.

Open one drawer, and click and reward when your dog looks at it.

Click and reward when your dog approaches the drawer to check it out.

Wait for your dog to touch the drawer with either his nose or foot, depending on your preference for him. Click and reward when he touches it with the appropriate body part. If needed, you can tap or put a target on the drawer to encourage him to touch it.

Click and treat any push by your dog on the drawer. He may be tentative at first, so praise effusively when he does push it.

Work up to your dog pushing the drawer all the way closed. You can now add in your verbal cue by saying "Close it" before letting him go to the drawer. Only reward when he closes the drawer completely.

Open and Close Doors

Verbal Cue	Prerequisites
"Open" and "Slam"	None
Hand Signal	Tools
None	Any door

Your dog can easily learn to open and close doors on command. This trick comes in handy if you have your arms full and need the door opened all the way and then closed behind you. For training, choose a door that swings easily on its hinges. You can then work up to a stickier door.

DOG TREAT

If your dog has a short, wide muzzle, it may be difficult for him to use his nose to nudge a door open. Instead, you can teach him to use his paw. Click and reward first when he touches the door with his paw at all, and then when his paw touches the edge of the door. From there, you can work up to him pulling the door open with his paw. If necessary, use a target to draw his attention to the door.

Open the Door

Position the door so it is only open a few inches. Click and reward when your dog looks at or approaches the door.

Click and reward when your dog touches the door with his nose.

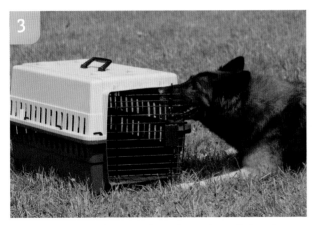

Wait until your dog touches the edge of the door or the space between the door and the frame to click and reward. Repeat until he is consistently touching this part of the door.

OPENING THE DOOR BOTH WAYS

Once your dog has mastered opening the door by pulling it, go to the other side (or send him inside the crate) and practice pushing it. This direction is easier for many dogs because they can use their whole head and body to push open the door.

Click and reward when your dog nudges the door with his nose. You can now add in your verbal cue by saying "Open" and then rewarding when he nudges the door. You can then gradually increase how much your dog has to open the door to get a reward.

Close the Door

Position the door so it is only open a few inches. Click and reward when your dog looks at or approaches the door.

Click and reward when your dog touches the door with his nose. Repeat until he is consistently touching the door.

DOG TREAT

Your dog can only close a door all the way from one side—the side that he can push on. If you want to teach him to go through a door and then close it so the door is between you, find a Dutch door to practice with. Send your dog through the door, and then click and reward when he pushes it closed. The Dutch door allows you to lean over and reward your dog even with the door closed in between you. When your dog has mastered the Dutch door, you can try closing a regular solid door.

CLOSING THE DOOR USING HIS PAW

Your dog can close a door using his paws, too. Click and reward when he touches the door with his paw instead of his nose, and then work through the remaining steps. You can even teach your dog to jump up with both paws to push the door closed, but if your dog tends to get excited and use a lot of force when jumping, we recommend you stick with the nose method.

Wait until your dog pushes on the door to click and reward. Repeat until he moves the door a little with every try.

TROUBLESHOOTING

If you taught your dog to open a door first, he may have some trouble closing it initially. When you start teaching him to close a door, brace the door with your foot or a stopper to prevent him from opening it. You can then reward him for touching the side of the door rather than the edge. Once he has learned both behaviors, you can test the verbal cues by asking him to do one or the other. Only reward if he does what you asked him to do—if he doesn't, just try again.

Work up to your dog pushing the door all the way closed. Add in your verbal cue by saying "Slam" and then rewarding when the door clicks closed.

Pull Up a Blanket

This trick teaches your dog to pull up a blanket to keep you warm on a cold day. It is perfect for when the blanket is on the far end of the couch and you don't want to stand up to get it. Plus, most dogs enjoy any excuse to be silly with their owners.

Verbal Cue	Prerequisites
"Get the blanket"	Fetch, Hold, Carry
Hand Signal	Tools
	Blanket

! PET PAUSE

Don't use fancy or delicate blankets for this trick. Even if your dog doesn't mean to, his teeth could damage delicate fabric.

Sit and place a blanket or towel by your feet. Click and reward when your dog investigates the blanket. Repeat several times to reinforce that you want him to interact with the blanket.

Wait until your dog grabs at the blanket to click and reward. Use your Fetch command to help him out if he seems confused. Repeat until he is consistently grabbing the blanket.

DOG TREAT

If you want to be more specific, you can teach your dog to grab the blanket by an edge. There are three ways to do this: use a blanket with a distinctive border and only reward when your dog touches or grabs the border, knot a corner of the blanket and only reward when he grabs the knot, or always start out with the blanket folded so a corner is at the top and then reward when he touches or grabs the corner.

Encourage your dog to bring the blanket to you. Click and reward for any progress, even if he only makes one step toward you while holding the blanket. Use Hold and Carry as extra clues for your dog.

Work up to your dog bringing the blanket all the way to you. You can now add in your verbal cue by saying "Get the blanket" before or as you signal him to get it.

Perch

Verbal Cue	Prerequisites
"Perch," "Get up," "Step"	Sit, Down, Back Up
Hand Signal	Tools
None	Perch

Perching covers anytime your dog puts two or more of his feet on a raised object. This trick can help improve balance and coordination, and can be done with objects in a wide range of shapes and sizes. Your perch just needs to be appropriate for the size of your dog and able to support his weight. When first starting out, we recommend you use a very low perch that is easy for your dog to step up on.

Basic Perching

Click and reward when your dog looks at the perch. You can point at it to help him out if needed.

Click and reward when your dog touches the perch. At this point, he can use either his nose or paw.

Require your dog to touch the perch with his paw before you click and reward. Repeat until he is consistently touching the top of the perch with his paw.

ADVANCED PERCHING

Once your dog has mastered perching, you can teach him to turn in a circle while keeping his paws on the perch. To do this, use a lure to lead his head around to the side. When he moves his hind feet, praise. Gradually work up to a complete turn in both directions. If he ever loses his balance and steps off, tell him to Perch and try again.

Wait until your dog puts both of his front paws on the perch to click and reward. Repeat until he consistently steps up with both front paws. You can now add in your verbal cue by telling him to "Perch" before he steps up on the perch.

Perching with All Four Feet

Using a larger perch, encourage your dog to jump up with all four of his feet. Use a different verbal cue, such as "Get up." Repeat until he jumps onto the perch on your command.

If there is enough room, you can ask your dog to Sit or Down on the perch.

Hind Foot Perching

Stand your dog at the bottom of a staircase. Click and reward when he touches the bottom step with a hind foot.

Click and reward when your dog steps up on the step with one hind foot. You may need to help him by telling him to Back Up. Repeat until he is easily stepping up with one foot.

Wait until both hind feet are on top of the bottom step to click and reward. Add in your verbal cue by saying "Step" before he steps up. Repeat until he is easily stepping onto the step on command.

COMBINATION PERCHING

Once your dog has mastered perching with both his front and hind feet, you can use multiple perches to have your dog balance between the two. This may look like your dog is doing yoga!

Switch over to using a smaller perch. Be patient, as it will take some adjusting for your dog to figure out how to fit his feet on the smaller perch.

Speak

Speak is the perfect trick for noisy dogs who love to bark. It can also help build confidence in quiet, more timid dogs who are shy in public. It's a good idea to have your dog know both this and Quiet, a trick we will talk about later in this book.

Verbal Cue	Prerequisites
"Get loud"	None
Hand Signal	**Tools**
None	None

PET PAUSE

If you live in an apartment or townhouse with neighbors close by, this trick may not be a good option for you and your dog. Be considerate of your neighbors and don't encourage your dog to make lots of unnecessary noise.

One way to help with this is to teach your dog that he will only be rewarded for Speak if he barks a single time when asked. To do this, be very consistent after adding in your verbal cue and only reward your dog for a single bark. If he barks more than once or barks without being asked, ignore him.

Click and reward for any noise your dog makes. To encourage him to bark, get him excited by playing with him or talking in an excited voice.

Require an actual bark before you click and reward. Repeat several times to reinforce that you want a full bark.

Add in your verbal cue by saying "Get loud" and then rewarding for the bark. Reward your dog only when he barks on command, and not when he barks on his own. Repeat until he consistently barks when you ask him to.

TEACHING "WHISPER"

As well as teaching the full bark, you can also teach your dog to whisper by just doing a little woof. To teach this, reward for the soft woof and then pair that with your "Whisper" command.

Quiet

Verbal Cue	Prerequisites
"Shhh"	None
Hand Signal	Tools
	None

Quiet is a good companion trick for Speak, but also works for any chronically noisy dog. Because this trick is all about the absence of sound, rather than the action of barking, it can take longer for dogs to figure out what you want. To make the process a little clearer to your dog, we recommend you teach your dog to close his mouth rather than just stop barking.

PET PAUSE

If it is really hot out and your dog is panting, don't require him to close his mouth for long. Praise him for a few seconds of Quiet and then calmly release him. Even a short Quiet will help to break off his focus on whatever he was barking at and refocus his attention on you.

1

Click and reward when your dog closes his mouth. Repeat until he figures out what you are rewarding him for and starts to close his mouth on purpose.

2

Add in your verbal cue. Say "Shhh," give your hand signal, and then click and reward when your dog closes his mouth.

Gradually increase the length of time your dog has to keep his mouth closed to get a reward.

DOG TREAT

At first, practice this trick in a calm, quiet location so it is easy for your dog to also be quiet and calm. Once he has mastered Quiet in that setting, take him somewhere more exciting and where he is more likely to bark. You can also test his knowledge of Quiet by telling him to Speak and then to be quiet.

To help encourage calmness, keep your praise and rewards calm. Pet him gently and tell him in a soft voice what a good dog he is instead of cheering and jumping around. This will help to keep him quiet as much as knowing the trick will. If using the clicker gets him too excited and causes him to bark, put it away and just use your voice as a marker instead.

Freeze

Verbal Cue	Prerequisites
"Freeze"	Wait
Hand Signal	Tools
None	None

Freeze is a fun game you can play with your dog that also expands on the self-control skills he learned when you taught him Wait. The difference between Freeze and Wait is that for Freeze, your dog will already be in motion and has to stop and stand still, rather than just maintaining a stationary position.

DOG TREAT

One way to help your dog understand this trick is to "freeze" yourself. Walk with your dog and then say "Freeze" and stop moving. Praise and reward when he also stops. This makes it more like a game, especially when you work up to asking your dog to stop from a full run—both of you can be running around having fun, and then Freeze before continuing to play. It is just like the kids' game "Red Light, Green Light."

Allow your dog to mill around the area where you are training. When he stops moving and stands, click and reward. Repeat a few times until he starts to stand still on purpose.

Add in your verbal cue by saying "Freeze" before your dog stops moving. Practice several times until he comes to a stop whenever he hears the word "Freeze."

Gradually extend the time he has to remain still before being released and rewarded.

COMBINING WITH OTHER TRICKS

You can also combine Freeze with other tricks that involve motion, such as Weave Through My Legs, Back Up, or any trick that involves sending your dog to something. Start the original trick, and then in the middle say "Freeze." Your dog should Freeze, and then you can release him to continue on with the original trick.

Up the ante by getting your dog moving faster before you tell him to Freeze. Start by getting him to trot, and then when he can do a Freeze from a trot, try it from a full run. Always release and reward after he has come to a standstill.

Push a Baby Carriage

Verbal Cue	Prerequisites
"Push"	None
Hand Signal	**Tools**
None	Carriage

Push a Baby Carriage is a cute trick to do with a wagon, carriage, or cart. Whatever you decide to use, make sure it is appropriate for your dog's size and rolls easily. Stuffed animals to ride along are totally optional!

DOG TREAT

Your dog may need to push on a specific area of the carriage to make it move. If so, reward your dog a few times for touching the carriage anywhere with his nose, and then only reward when he touches it in the location where he will need to push. Continue this as you work through the remaining steps. Another option is to teach your dog to grab the carriage's handle.

Click and reward when your dog looks at the carriage.

Click and reward when your dog touches the carriage. Repeat a few times until your dog is readily touching the carriage with his nose.

Wait until your dog actually pushes the carriage to click and reward. Repeat several times until he is consistently moving the carriage a little with each push.

Add in your verbal cue by saying "Push" before you let him go to the carriage.

Gradually increase the distance your dog can push the carriage.

Find the Hidden Treat

This scenting game exercises your dog's nose and mind. We used three metal tins with holes punched in the bottom to hide the treat, but you can also use cups, flower pots, or small boxes. Whichever you use, you will eventually be able to hide a treat inside and ask your dog to find it.

Verbal Cue	Prerequisites
"Find it"	None
Hand Signal	Tools
None	Tins

 DOG TREAT

The indication for the correct tin can be anything. Most dogs sniff or lick it, or you can teach your dog to grab or hit the correct tin. To do this, shape your dog to hit or grab it and then add your verbal cue and start letting him choose from multiple tins.

1	2
Open one of your tins and place a treat inside.	Send your dog to the open tin and let him eat the treat. This step shows him the tin has food inside.

Close the tin with the treat inside and tell your dog to "Find it." When he sniffs the tin, click and reward (you can either give him the treat in the tin or a different one). Repeat a few times, paying attention to how he sniffs or paws at the tin with the treat inside.

Place all three of your tins on the ground with a treat inside one. Tell your dog to "Find it," and reward when he indicates the correct tin.

Shuffle the tins so the one with the treat is in a different spot and send your dog again. He should be able to find the tin with the treat by sniffing each one!

PART 4:
Advanced
Tricks

Scent Discrimination

Verbal Cue	Prerequisites
"Find mine"	Fetch, Hold, Carry, Find the Hidden Treat

Hand Signal	Tools
None	Clothespins Peanut butter

The scenting ability of dogs is well known and well respected. Your dog may never need to sniff out drugs, cancer cells, or a lost person, but she can learn to find an object that smells like you. In this trick, we use clothespins and peanut butter, but you can use any set of household items your dog can easily pick up along with her favorite spreadable treat. Teaching Find the Hidden Treat first is a good way to get your dog accustomed to sniffing and choosing between objects.

Start with just one object. Ask your dog to Fetch it to get her accustomed to handling it.

Rub the object in your hands so it will smell like you.

Put a dab of peanut butter on the object. This gives your dog an immediate reward that she will also associate with your scent.

Place the scented and treat-coated object on the ground and hold your hand in front of your dog's nose to give her your scent. This will become important later on.

Send your dog to get the object. After she licks off the peanut butter, use your Hold and Carry commands to tell her to bring it back to you and reward her for doing so. Repeat until she automatically brings the object back after licking the peanut butter.

Put out a second object that has not been scented or baited and send your dog, always letting her sniff your hand first. She will probably check out both objects and then settle on the one with the peanut butter. Repeat until she consistently chooses the correct object and brings it back.

Set out several objects, still both scenting and baiting the one you want your dog to find. She may need to search longer, but she should bring back the object with the peanut butter.

Fade the use of the peanut butter by using less and less and then none at all. It is best to go back to only two objects at this point to make it easier—the correct one and one that has not been scented. Always let your dog sniff your hand before sending her.

Add in your verbal cue by telling your dog to "Find mine" before you send her to sniff the objects.

DOG TREAT

To make the scenting easier for your dog, have a different person touch the objects you don't want her to bring back so they don't smell like you. If you don't have a helper, put on a glove that belongs to someone else to put out the extra objects, only touching the correct one with your bare hand. If your dog ever brings back the wrong object, just try again. This trick is complex and will take a while for your dog to figure out.

10

Work back up to having several choices your dog can choose between.

INDICATING AN OBJECT

If your dog just doesn't like to pick up things, you can teach her to indicate the correct object by touching it with her nose or paw instead. Teach the indication when working on step 5 by waiting for her to indicate the object after she licks off the peanut butter. Continue that through the remaining steps, so that instead of finding the object and bringing it back, your dog will find the object and then indicate it.

Search for an Object

Verbal Cue	Prerequisites
"Where's your __?"	Fetch
Hand Signal	Tools
None	Toy 

This trick is neat because it teaches your dog both the name of a specific object and how to actively search for that object. Once your dog has learned to search for one object when asked, you can add other items to his vocabulary. We used a toy turtle, so the verbal cue is, "Where's your turtle?"

DOG TREAT

If your dog is not toy motivated and would prefer treats, give her a food reward when she brings the toy to you. She will learn to retrieve the toy because she can then trade it in for a treat!

Have your dog Fetch the toy.

Switch to your verbal cue by asking your dog "Where's your turtle?" before you let her get the toy. Repeat several times to get her used to the pattern of retrieving the turtle after hearing that command.

Hide the toy in an obvious place, such as under or behind something. Let your dog watch you hide the toy. Ask her where it is and then play with her a little when she finds it and brings it back. Repeat two or three times.

Now hide the toy in a similar place, but without your dog watching. Ask her to search for it and praise when she finds it.

Hide the toy in a more difficult place, or somewhere that has more places where it could be hiding. Praise and play when she finds the toy!

Hold an Object with Your Paw

This challenging trick requires your dog to hold an object to her body. We used a plastic water bottle, but many objects will work, such as a shoe or teddy bear.

Verbal Cue	Prerequisites
"Grip"	None
Hand Signal	Tools
None	Water bottle

DOG TREAT

Smooth objects are a little more difficult to use for this trick because the slippery surface makes them harder to hold onto. If you're using a slippery object, you may need to help your dog out by adjusting the object a little when she grabs it.

Have your water bottle and clicker in one hand and your reward in the other. If you can't manage both clicker and bottle, just use your voice as a marker instead.

Hold the bottle in front of your dog and click and reward when she touches it. She can use her nose or paw at this point.

Wait until your dog raises her paw to click and reward. Repeat a few times until she is consistently touching the bottle with her paw.

Require your dog to wrap her paw around the bottle before you click and reward. You may need to adjust and hold the bottle closer to her body. When she is wrapping her paw around it consistently, add in your verbal cue by telling her to "Grip."

Gradually extend the length of time your dog holds the position and let go with your hand so she is holding the bottle unassisted.

Treat on Your Nose

Verbal Cue	Prerequisites
"Wait"	Wait, Leave It
Hand Signal	**Tools**
None	None

This classic trick requires lots of self-control on the part of your dog. It is an advanced version of the behavior Wait because your dog will need to hold her position while resisting the temptation of the treat on her nose. To help her, we recommend using a bland biscuit instead of a really tasty treat to start off.

DOG TREAT

Never let your dog eat the treat if she drops it before you verbally release her. If she does cheat, tell her to Leave It and grab the treat yourself. This will teach her that she has to wait, but if she does what you ask, she will get to eat the treat eventually. She may even figure out how to flip the treat and catch it when you release her!

Gently hold your dog's muzzle and place a treat on her nose. While still holding her muzzle, tell her to "Wait" and praise her. Say "Okay!" to release her, let go, and give her the treat. Repeat until she relaxes with the treat on her nose.

Tell your dog to "Wait" or "Leave it" and try to let go of her muzzle for a second or two. If she moves and the treat falls, grab it and try again.

3

Gradually increase the amount of time your dog will stay still, unassisted, with the treat on her nose. Always give her a release word like "Okay!" to let her know when she can eat the treat!

COMBINING WITH OTHER TRICKS

You can combine Treat on Your Nose with other stationary tricks, such as Sit, Down, or even Sit Pretty!

Bang-Bang, You're Dead

Verbal Cue	Prerequisites
"Bang!"	Down
Hand Signal	**Tools**
	None

Bang-Bang, You're Dead is another classic trick that everyone loves to see. Once you teach your dog the basics, you can add a little flair to make your rendition of the "kill shot" more special.

DOG TREAT

Once your dog has mastered Bang-Bang, You're Dead, you can try having her do it from a sitting or standing position, or even when she is moving (when she hears "Bang!" she should stop and drop to the ground). You can also teach her to lay her head flat on the ground by only rewarding when she puts her head down while lying on her side.

Tell your dog to Down.

Lure her so she will lie on her side by leading her nose toward her tail and a little over her back. Reward when she is flat on her side. Repeat until she is flopping over with minimal assistance.

Give your hand signal and say "Bang!" before you lure her onto her side.

ADDING "CPR"

One fun way to release your dog at the end of this trick is to pretend to give her CPR. To teach this, remind your dog to Wait, and then gently press on her side two or three times. When you're done, jump up and cheer, encouraging your dog to do the same. You can also ask her to Wait while you pretend to check for a pulse or listen for breathing.

Gradually fade the lure until your dog will flop onto her side when she sees the signal and hears "Bang!"

Backward Crawl

Verbal Cue	Prerequisites
"Flee!"	Down
Hand Signal	**Tools**
	None

Crawling backward is a fun skill that many dogs enjoy. You can use a silly command, such as "Danger! Flee!" or "Duck and cover!" along with your hand cue to make the trick more exciting to spectators. Crawling backward is not a natural movement for most dogs, so expect your dog to take some time to learn this trick.

TROUBLESHOOTING

If your dog gets up from the Down position, just remind her to Down and don't reward her until she does it correctly. You can also carefully start out with your dog under a table or chair so she has to scoot backward without getting up, and then fade the table or chair as she understands the physical action you want.

Put your dog in a Down position.

Using a treat or toy as a lure, draw your dog's nose down between her front legs toward her chest. This will cause her to scoot backward. Praise, click if using a clicker, and reward.

DOG TREAT

You can also work on increasing the distance that your dog crawls backward away from you. To do this, require your dog to do multiple scoots backward without you moving toward her. At first, just ask for two scoots away, and then reward. You can then gradually work up to larger distances. To reinforce motion away from you, toss a treat or toy to or behind your dog when rewarding her.

Repeat several times and work on fading the lure. You can fade the lure to a shooing motion with your fingers or hands, signaling her to go backward. This will become your hand signal. You can also step toward her as another hint.

When your dog can scoot backward without a lure, add in your verbal cue by saying "Flee!" before you give your signal. You can now start asking for multiple scoots, which will look like your dog is crawling backward!

Dance on Your Hind Legs

Dance on Your Hind Legs takes the trick Stand on Your Hind Legs and adds motion so your dog is dancing! This trick is fun at backyard parties and when celebrating good news.

Verbal Cue	Prerequisites
"Dance"	Stand on Your Hind Legs
Hand Signal	Tools
	None

Review Stand on Your Hind Legs with your dog.

Use a lure to encourage your dog to move around and spin in a circle while on her hind legs. If she drops down on all fours, just ask her to stand up again. Repeat until she is easily moving around on her hind legs.

Add in your verbal cue by saying "Dance" before you lure your dog.

DOG TREAT

As well as jumping around at random, you can formally combine this trick with Spin and Twirl. Just go through the steps to teach those tricks, this time requiring your dog to be on her hind legs. Dance on Your Hind Legs can also be combined with Back Up and Side Pass. When teaching any of these, your dog will probably drop down onto all fours frequently during training. This will happen less as she figures out what you want and is less confused.

Fade the lure and use of a treat until your dog dances after being given the hand signal and verbal cue.

Dunk It

Verbal Cue	Prerequisites
"Dunk it"	Hold, Carry, Give, Drop It
Hand Signal	**Tools**
None	Basketball hoop Ball

Having your dog "dunk it" will delight friends of all ages—especially basketball fans. This is a complicated trick that requires your dog to master a couple of skills. First, you teach your dog to dunk her head into the basketball hoop; then, you add the ball to the picture.

Click and reward when your dog approaches the hoop.

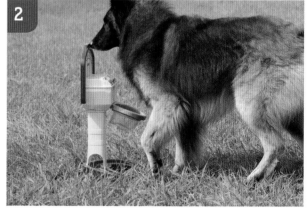

Click and reward when your dog touches any part of the hoop. Repeat two or three times to make sure she gets the connection.

Wait until your dog touches the rim of the hoop with her nose to click and reward. Repeat until she is consistently touching the rim.

Click and reward when she puts her nose over the center of the rim.

Wait for your dog to dip her muzzle into the net to click and reward. Repeat until she is consistently dunking. You can now add in your verbal cue by saying "Dunk it" before you let her go to the hoop.

Ask your dog to Hold the ball.

Tell your dog to Carry the ball toward you and the hoop. If she drops the ball, ask her to pick it up again and remind her to Hold.

Hold your hand under the hoop so your dog can see it, and ask her to Give you the ball. Repeat until she consistently places the ball in your hand through the hoop.

Fade the use of your hand, now telling your dog to Drop the ball when she is holding it over the hoop. Repeat until your dog drops the ball through the hoop without your hand present.

DOG TREAT

If your dog is hesitant to put her nose in the rim of the basket, you can hold your hand under it and ask her to Touch. Repeat that a few times until she is comfortable, and then try asking her to do it on her own.

Bring back your "Dunk it" command by telling your dog to Dunk It when she approaches the hoop with the ball. It's a slam dunk!

TROUBLESHOOTING

This trick has a lot of different parts, which means there are many places where your dog can get confused. This is especially true when working with the ball. If your dog is already highly excited about the ball, put away your clicker and just use your voice as a marker to make that part of training a little calmer. You can also toss the ball as your reward, as long as your dog will bring it back. Be patient, as the later steps of training will take several sessions to perfect.

If at any point your dog hits the basketball hoop with her paw, just ignore her and try again. Do the same thing if she throws the ball at you—ignore her, don't allow her to play with the ball, and then remind her to Hold the ball.

Skateboard

Verbal Cue	Prerequisites
"Ride it"	Perch

Hand Signal	Tools
None	Skateboard

This trick appeals to two groups of dogs—the very active dog who wants to fly around on the skateboard, and the sedate dog who simply wants to ride. This is best taught through shaping, though you may have to lure or encourage your dog to approach and put her paws on the board.

Click and reward when your dog looks at or approaches the skateboard. You may need to point to it or place a treat on it if she does not show any interest. Moving it a little bit yourself may also attract your dog.

Brace the skateboard so it won't move, and click and reward when your dog touches it. At first, reward any touch—nose or paw. You can then hold out for a paw touch.

3

Wait until your dog puts one paw on the skateboard to click and reward.

4

Require two paws to be on the board before your dog gets a reward. If you have already taught Perch, this step should come quickly.

5

Encourage your dog to put all of her paws on the board. Allow the board to move a little, but stay close and support her. Give lots of praise and rewards when the skateboard starts to move. Repeat until she is comfortable getting on the board.

6

Add in your verbal cue by telling your dog to "Ride it" before she hops on the board.

DOG TREAT

It is okay if your dog jumps off the skateboard! If your dog doesn't feel trapped on the board, she will be more comfortable with it and get used to the motion faster. At first, she may only stay on the board for a few seconds. Be patient, and gradually work up to having her stay on the board for a longer amount of time. Use lots of praise to calm her and let her know that she is doing a great job.

7

Encourage your dog to move the skateboard herself. Some dogs use one paw to push themselves along, while others leap on after a running start. Reward for either method.

SKATEBOARDING VARIATION

If your dog likes to chase, you can use that instinct to your advantage. Roll the skateboard slowly and click and reward when your dog follows it, gradually working up to her putting a paw or two on the board and then hopping on.

Be sure to only reward her for "catching" the board with her paws—never reward for grabbing at it with her mouth. Grabbing could result in injuries to your dog's teeth and is also counterproductive. She will progress faster if she realizes from the start that only using her paws will earn a treat.

Play Soccer

Verbal Cue	Prerequisites
"Get it"	Touch
Hand Signal	Tools
None	Soccer ball

Playing soccer is a great way to exercise your dog, plus she will love it! For most dogs, the act of playing and moving the ball is a reward in itself. We recommend using a ball that is sturdy enough to handle some abuse and won't pop if your dog hits it with a tooth or nail. An actual soccer ball works great.

DOG TREAT

Your dog can also use her paws to play soccer by hitting the ball like a person would. The object of the game is for your dog to return the ball to you without picking it up in her mouth. If your dog tends to try to pick the ball up, find a bigger one she won't be able to fit in her mouth.

Hold your hand against the ball and tell your dog to Touch. Repeat two or three times to show her what you want.

Remove your hand and reward when your dog touches the ball on her own. Repeat until she is consistently touching the ball with her nose.

Require your dog to push the ball so it moves before you reward. Position yourself so she is pushing the ball toward you.

Add in your verbal cue by saying "Get it" before your dog pushes the ball. Gradually extend the distance she pushes it toward you.

Now you're ready to play! Kick the soccer ball and send your dog to bring it back.

Go Out and Circle

Verbal Cue	Prerequisites
"Go 'round"	None
Hand Signal	Tools
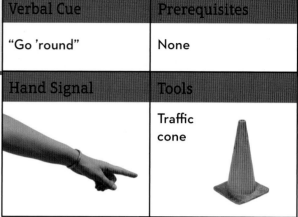	Traffic cone

This is a fun trick to impress friends but also can help you and your dog with everyday obstacles. (Remember the last time you got your dog's leash tangled around a light pole?) We used a traffic cone to teach this trick, but you can use just about any object that you have on hand.

CIRCLING FROM EACH SIDE

Like humans, most dogs are "sided" and will prefer to turn one way or the other when circling the cone or other object. Once your dog has mastered circling in the direction she prefers, work on teaching her to go the other way as well. You may need to spend extra time on the earlier steps when working on her harder side.

Place the cone a short distance away and draw your dog's attention to it.

Use a treat or toy to lure your dog around the cone. Reward when she has completed the rotation. Repeat a few times until she is readily circling the cone and doesn't need to be formally lured.

Add in your verbal cue by saying "Go 'round" before sending her around the cone.

Gradually increase the distance between you and the cone so you are sending your dog to circle it from farther away.

Dust

Verbal Cue	Prerequisites
"Dust it"	Fetch, Hold, Carry
Hand Signal	**Tools**
None	Duster

Having a dog who can help with household chores is both useful and fun. You may not want to trust your dog with dusting the heirloom china pieces, but she can do the dining room chairs. If nothing else, you will impress your friends and relatives!

> **! PET PAUSE**
>
> Never leave the duster with your dog unsupervised or allow her to play with or chew on it. Otherwise, she could accidentally ingest feathers.

Click and reward when your dog touches the duster with her nose. Repeat two or three times to reinforce that you want her to touch the duster.

Wait until your dog grabs the duster with her mouth to click and reward. Repeat until she is consistently grabbing the duster. For now, don't worry about where on the duster she grabs.

Require your dog to grab the duster by the handle before you click and reward, working up to her lifting it by the handle. Repeat until she consistently lifts the duster by the handle.

Encourage your dog to carry the duster over to a chair or other piece of furniture, reminding her to Hold and/or Carry. If she drops the duster, ask her to pick it up and try again. Repeat until she can easily walk with the duster.

Click and reward when your dog actually touches the chair with the duster. You can now add in your verbal cue by telling her to "Dust it" before she approaches the chair. Repeat until she consistently rubs the duster over furniture, and gradually work on increasing the duration.

Mop

Verbal Cue	Prerequisites
"Clean up"	Targeting

Hand Signal	Tools
None	Rag

Asking your dog to help you Mop makes cleaning day a little more fun; you can even make her clean up some of her own messes. You can use any rag or small towel for this trick. Paper towels would also work but have the potential to shred if your dog is enthusiastic about her cleaning duties!

DOG TREAT

The hardest part of this trick is getting your dog to move the rag. If your dog is having trouble, get her really excited by talking in an excited voice and giving her a running start to the rag. You can also race her to the rag. The momentum behind her approach should make the rag slide!

Place the rag on a smooth surface and click and reward when your dog looks at it.

Click and reward when your dog touches the rag with either her nose or paw. Repeat two or three times to reinforce she is supposed to interact with the rag.

Wait until she touches the rag with her paw to click and reward. Repeat until she is consistently using her paw.

Click and reward only if she moves the rag with her paw. This can be either a dragging motion by pulling the rag toward her, or a pushing motion by pouncing on the rag and sliding it on the floor.

Add in your verbal cue by saying "Clean up" before she puts her paw on the rag and then rewarding when she wipes the floor.

Put the Toilet Seat Down

Verbal Cue	Prerequisites
"Seat down"	None
Hand Signal	**Tools**
None	Toilet with a lid

It can be difficult to get people to put the toilet seat down, so having a dog who can do this is very impressive. You can use any toilet with a lid, be it a regular toilet, child training toilet, or portable camping one.

! PET PAUSE

If you're working with a real porcelain toilet, apply some foam padding to the underside of the seat or lid to soften the fall. Loud crashes are not good for the toilet and could also scare your dog.

1 Encourage your dog to approach the toilet and click and reward when she looks at or touches it. Repeat a few times to reinforce this behavior.

2 Require your dog to touch the back of the raised lid or seat before you click and reward. Depending on your dog's size, she can use either her nose or paw. Repeat until she is consistently touching the raised seat.

Wait for your dog to push on the lid to click and reward. At this point, reward for any movement. Repeat until she is moving the lid a little every time.

USING A TARGET

You can also use a target to teach this trick. Place the target on the toilet where you will want your dog to push with her nose or paw and ask her to touch it. You can even tape the target in place so your dog can learn the entire trick while still using the target. You can then gradually fade the use of the target until your dog can put the toilet seat down unassisted.

Require your dog to fully close the lid before you click and reward. You can now add in your verbal cue by telling her "Seat down" before she approaches the toilet.

Alphabet

Verbal Cue	Prerequisites
"B" (can vary by the letters you're using)	None
Hand Signal	**Tools**
None	At least two letters of the alphabet

Your dog will look like a true genius when she picks out the letter of her own name! We used wooden block letters, but you can also use pieces of cardboard with the letters stenciled on. Make sure that the letters you are using are clear and distinctive.

DOG TREAT

Once your dog has mastered identifying one letter, you can go back and teach her the name of additional letters. You can also use numbers to show off her "math skills."

1 Place the letter near your dog where she can reach it. Click and reward if she looks at the letter. If she is having trouble, you can point to help her out.

2 Click and reward when she approaches the letter.

Wait until your dog touches the letter with either her nose or paw to click. Decide which action you (or your dog) prefer and only reward for that behavior. This will eventually be your dog's indication of what letter she is choosing, so it needs to be consistent.

When your dog reliably touches the letter, add in the name of that letter as your verbal cue. Repeat several times until she understands the connection.

Add a second letter to test your dog. Try one with a different shape so it will be easier for her to tell them apart. Use the verbal cue for the original letter, and reward when she finds it! Repeat until she consistently indicates the correct letter on command.

Put Your Toys in the Basket

Verbal Cue	Prerequisites
"Get your toys"	Fetch, Drop It
Hand Signal	**Tools**
	Toy basket

Does your dog like to spread her toys all over the house? She can learn to put them away, too! This trick is an advanced form of Fetch. After retrieving one toy, you can then send her to get more until all of the toys have been returned to the basket.

DOG TREAT

If your dog is highly toy motivated, she may focus in on the first toy she brings you and want to play instead of getting more. Be patient and cover the toy or hide it behind your back if needed. Never let her steal the toy back out of the basket. When she gives up and Fetches a second toy, play with her a little as a reward.

Place a toy on the ground and tell your dog to Fetch it.

When she gets close to you with the toy, hold out the basket so it is under her head and tell her to Drop It. If she misses the basket, ask her to pick the toy back up and try again.

PUTTING AWAY LAUNDRY

You can also do this trick with clothing items. Teach your dog to Fetch different types of clothes, and then go through the steps for putting them in a basket. Use "Laundry" as your verbal cue to tell her you want her to bring you clothes instead of toys.

Once the first toy is in the basket, send your dog to Fetch another one.

Repeat until your dog is aiming for the basket on her own when she collects her toys. You can now add in your verbal cue by telling her to "Get your toys."

Roll Up in a Blanket

Verbal Cue	Prerequisites
"Get it; roll"	Roll Over, Hold
Hand Signal	Tools
	Blanket

Roll Up in a Blanket is the perfect trick to end your day, especially if you have a short-haired dog that gets cold in the winter! Choose a blanket that is big enough for your dog and sturdy enough to handle being grabbed, and then you are ready to get started.

THE HAND SIGNAL

Using the Roll Over hand signal gives your dog some extra clues as to what you want her to do. This is especially helpful in the early stages when your dog is confused about the blanket. As she masters the trick, you may find that you no longer need a formal hand signal and that she responds to the verbal cue combined with the visual aid of the blanket.

1 Review Roll Over with your dog. Pay attention to which direction she usually rolls.

2 Tell your dog to Down on the blanket, lying close to one edge. The main part of the blanket should be to the side your dog will roll.

3

Draw your dog's attention to the corner of the blanket, and click and reward when she touches it. Repeat until she can touch the corner without assistance.

4

Click and reward when your dog grabs the corner of the blanket. Add in the "Get it" part of your verbal cue before she grabs the corner each time. Repeat until she consistently grabs and lifts the corner.

5

Tell your dog to Hold the corner, and work up to her Holding it for several seconds. Working on the Hold now will make it easier for her to complete the trick.

DOG TREAT

If your dog is having trouble finding the corner of the blanket, knot the corner to make it more obvious and easier to grab.

With your dog holding the corner of the blanket, ask her to Roll Over. At first, she may drop the corner or stop partway through the roll. Praise and try again with an extra reminder to Hold.

Work up to a complete Roll Over with the blanket held in your dog's mouth.

GIVING THE VERBAL CUE

Because this trick has multiple parts, it is best to give your verbal cue with a small pause in the middle that gives your dog time to locate and grab the corner of the blanket before she is told to Roll Over. As your dog gains more experience with this trick, she won't need as much of a pause.

You can also further condense your verbal cue by using a completely different command that encompasses the whole trick rather than each part. First, choose your command, like "Cozy" or "Pigs in blankets." Go through the steps to teach your dog the entire trick, and then add in your new verbal cue before sending her to the blanket. To teach your dog the new verbal cue is equivalent to "Get it" plus "Roll," say your verbal cue and then pause before giving the old cues. As you practice, she will start to anticipate and respond to the new verbal cue before you can even say the old ones. From then on, you can just use the single cue!

8

Fade out the Hold command in the middle of the trick and put the two main parts together. Your dog should grab the corner of the blanket when she hears "Get it" and roll over when she hears "Roll" right after.

PART 5:
Appendixes

Glossary

behavior   Something your dog does; an action. Behaviors can be automatic or learned.

carry   When your dog holds an object in his mouth while moving without dropping it.

clicker   A training tool that makes a clicking sound and can be used to mark correct behaviors.

down   A stationary position where your dog's whole body is lowered to the ground.

drop it   A verbal cue that tells your dog to drop an object held in his mouth.

fade   Making a visual guide or signal smaller or less obvious gradually over time so your dog no longer needs it.

give   A verbal cue that tells your dog to deliver an object to your hands and let go of it.

hand signal   The hand motion your dog will associate with a specific trick or behavior. Dogs are excellent at reading body language, so hand signals can be subtle.

hold   When your dog keeps an object in his mouth and doesn't drop it.

lure   Something that your dog likes and that can be used to lead your dog through an action or into a position. The most common lures are toys or food treats.

luring   A method of training where you guide your dog into the desired position or action using food or a toy. Lures will eventually be faded out when your dog learns the behavior.

marker   Something that indicates when your dog is doing something right. This can be your voice (such as saying "yes") or a sound (such as using a clicker).

positive reinforcement   Giving a reward for doing something right; the addition of something your dog likes.

release   A verbal cue that tells your dog he is done with what he was doing and can move about freely. Many trainers use "okay" or "free."

reward   Something your dog likes that can be used to motivate him during training. A reward can be food, toys, or play and praise.

shaping   A training method in which your dog guesses what you want him to do and you reward him for being on the right track. Your dog will gradually have to increase his effort to get a reward.

sit   A stationary position with your dog's hind end on the ground and front legs upright.

target   A flat training tool, often a jar lid or something similar. Your dog is taught to touch it or is sent to it from a distance.

treat   Any food item your dog can safely eat that you use as a reward during training.

trick   A behavior or combination of behaviors that is fun and often a little silly.

verbal cue   The voice command your dog will associate with a specific trick or behavior.

wait   A verbal cue that tells your dog to stay where he is or hold the position he is in.

Resources

The books and websites mentioned here can help you round out your dog's education and your own. Learning how your dog learns and how to train will help strengthen the bond between you and your dog.

Books

Book, Mandy, and Cheryl Smith. *Right on Target!: Taking Dog Training to a New Level.* Chicago: Dogwise Publishing, 2006.

Cheryl Smith and Mandy Book are trainers who love to have fun while molding well-behaved canine companions.

Dennison, Pam. *The Complete Idiot's Guide to Positive Dog Training, Third Edition.* Indianapolis: Alpha Books, 2011.

Pam Dennison is known for using positive techniques to train and reform dogs. Her methods are fun for both you and your dog.

Palika, Liz. *Idiot's Guides: Dog Training.* Indianapolis: Alpha Books, 2013.

Liz Palika is a well-respected trainer and author. Her commonsense guidelines will help you to train your dog.

Pryor, Karen. *Getting Started: Clicker Training for Dogs.* Surrey: Ringpress Books, 2002.

Karen Pryor is the first lady of clicker training. She took scientific principles and made them work for real life with real people and real animals.

———. *Don't Shoot the Dog!: The New Art of Teaching and Training.* Gloucestershire: Ringpress Books, 2002.

This is the "bible" of clicker training from author Karen Pryor. It is not strictly about dogs, so feel free to use the techniques on your family and friends.

Websites

American Kennel Club
akc.org

While best known for its involvement with pure-bred dogs, the AKC's website has a wealth of information about all dogs, not just purebreds.

Association of Professional Dog Trainers
apdt.com

APDT is the base organization for positive trainers.

Karen Pryor Clicker Training
clickertraining.com/dog-training

Karen Pryor is the trainer who made clicker training a household phenomenon. Her website explains the theory behind shaping and clicker training and provides many resources and insights.

Trick Dog Titles
domorewithyourdog.com/pages/trickdogtitle.html

This is for those who want to go a step further and show that their dog does indeed have a diploma and just may be "smarter than your honor student."

Index

W–X–Y–Z